Letters to the Finishers
(who struggle to finish)

Finish Well!

Carl Dee

Letters to the Finishers
(who struggle to finish)

Candace E. Wilkins

New Season
BOOKS AND MEDIA

LETTERS TO THE FINISHERS
(who struggle to finish)

© 2019 Candace Wilkins

NewSeason Books and Media, LLC
PO Box 1403
Havertown, PA 19083
www.nsbooksandmedia.com

ISBN: 978-1-7336472-1-2

Table of Contents

Dedication

This book is lovingly dedicated to the mother of my birth (Linda Frazier), the mother of my heart (Betty Jean Scott), and the father I never got a chance to know (Nicholas Lance Tucker). Also, to my mother-in-law, Alice (Tucom) Wilkins-White. I promise to keep my promise to you. I hope I've made you all proud with the woman I am and am becoming.

INTRODUCTION
I Am Not a Finisher

"All my life, I had to fight..."
Sofia, *The Color Purple*

Dear Finisher,

I hope I finish this book.

Seriously!

I have a problem with completing projects I start. I struggle with finishing one thing before I'm on to the next one. I don't close cabinets. I sometimes don't flush the toilet (don't judge me). I hardly ever put items back where I get them. I tell my husband that my mind moves at 100 mph, and before I ever get done, in my mind, I already am. But ultimately, these trivial things would seem innocuous if it wasn't such a pervasive problem shadowing every endeavor of my whole life.

Yeah, I know. Dramatic much, Candace?

If I'm honest, I am jealous of people who seem to be able to see things through. How do they do that? How do they start something, breathe it every day, and see it through until completion? It seems like a superhuman ability, one that I don't have. Or at least, I didn't think I had. The last year has been an exercise in being consistent and finishing what I start. Not being shamed into finishing (been there). Not being scared into finishing (done that). Not being paid menial wages to finish (bought the T-shirt with my menial wages). I wanted to be excited about a project that I wasn't receiving a paycheck for, breathe it day in and day out, go through the struggle, and still, somehow, finish. When I lamented to a friend how soul crushing this problem was, he told me, "That's the book you should write. That's your first book!" As much as I knew how much this subject might help people, I wondered if I would have the wherewithal to actually finish it. Could I finish a book about how I struggle to finish things? Could I pull this off? Had I walked through enough of my healing to offer help?

So, here's the thing: this book isn't just for you--it's for me, too! I'm not writing this as a "Follow me. I know the way!" treatise. I'm writing this as an "I'm still on the journey, and maybe I can scatter some breadcrumbs so we can both find our way out of this forest!" This is not a formula for finishing. I don't believe in formulas. We're all so different and so are our journeys. If you're looking for a five-point plan for finishing, return this book 'cause this ain't it. If anything, this book is a deep dive into *why* we struggle with finishing and what we can possibly do about it. It's exploratory. It's what has worked (and is working) for me. But more so, it's a chronicling of some of the things about myself I had to confront on the path. The truths I had to tell myself. There are some things in this book you will agree with and others you may not. This is my journey, one I'm still walking out. It's a journey I'm certain will be helpful for some, if not most, but it's not one you can put on like a hand me down and walk around with.

I'm a creative. I'm a visionary and a seer. I used to say to other people, "I see A, and I see Z. I can probably work through B, C, D, E, F, and G, but usually, that's right where I stop." I'd argue that I know who I am and I know who I am not. But check it…that was half the problem right there. One we'll explore in a later letter. H-Y seemed hopelessly overwhelming to me. I get bogged down in H-Y. I get tired in H-Y. I get bored in H-Y. I get distracted in H-Y. I take several naps in H-Y (I'm an expert napper). I eventually stop in H-Y. So while I can see Z (In other words, I know what I want the end result to be), I never actually *see* Z. The work and push-through required in H-Y hinders me in making it to Z.

Here's where this problem shows up in my life prominently and maybe you can relate. I want abs. A tight, rippling, crop-top worthy set of abs. I can see them. I can sometimes feel them. I just know my life will be complete if I get a six-pack. Hell, I'll settle for a two-pack at this point. I see A (my stomach currently), and I see Z (crop-top abs). And I've worked through B, C, D, E, F, and G. I've…ugh…worked out for a bit. I've done crunches. I've changed eating habits, and I regularly suck down spinach smoothies when I really want a pint of ice cream. But after a few weeks (even months) of all of this, I stop. I halt. I can't stick with it. I grab a family size bag of Doritos, go up a size in my jeans and say, "Screw it!" That *push through even when you don't feel like it to gain the ultimate goal* thing that some people have? Yeah, nah. Not my ministry. Or so I thought.

So the fact that you now have these letters in your hands is monumental. Because it means that finally, definitively, irreversibly, I have finished them. It means that I started something, pushed through my H-Y and my Z, and this book has come to fruition. And here's all the truth you need to know: If I, a finisher who has trouble finishing, can finish, there is **nothing** in this world that can stop YOU from doing so.

Except you.

With the love of a newly birthed finisher,

C.W.

P.S. What does H-Y look like for you? What do you find to be the hardest things to push through? Open your journal or the notes app on your phone and write it out in detail. May I recommend you keep your journal or notes app handy? You'll need them.

I

I *AM a* Finisher

"I believe in you and me..."
Whitney Houston

Dear Finisher,

I recently came to a revelation. My favorite verse in the Bible is Philippians 1:6. I like it in all versions, but let's look at it in the ESV.

> *"And I am sure of this, that He who began a good work in you will bring it to completion at the day of Jesus Christ."*

This is my life verse. I've always loved the idea that God was going to work out His good in me. Looking back now, I think I might have fallen in love with this verse because God was the one who was going to bring something to completion in me! At least he wasn't relying on ME to finish it!

Whew!

I didn't want God to rely on me to finish *anything* because, let's face it, I didn't have the best track record in that area. But what happens when God starts putting ideas and dreams in your head? What then? What does that do to those of us who struggle with finishing? For me, it meant a few things:

5

- I had high levels of anxiety before even starting.
- I would start vowing not stop *this time*, and then would beat myself ragged for doing so.
- I would convince myself that God didn't want me to start that idea.
- I would stare at all the ideas I had (that I never pursued for fear of stopping) and say phrases like "one day" or "not now."
- I would watch other people start and pursue their ideas and get jealous.
- I would watch people put out work, ideas, and projects that I'd thought of years before and get angry, then depressed.
- I stopped telling anyone about the ideas I had because I knew they might hold me accountable. I didn't want to fail them.
- I would try to force myself to change. That wouldn't last long.
- I would perform finishing while avoiding the work necessary to actually *be* a finisher.
- I would convince myself that if it was really a God idea, surely the Holy Spirit would enable me to do it. Since he didn't, it must not be a God idea.
- I was convinced that I had some type of irreversible factory defect.

Does any of this sound familiar? I'm sure you can add to this list yourself. Does any of this sound in any way productive?

Of course not.

If you've confronted any of these, take heart. We're all on the same road. The good news is you're not alone, and you can survive it. We aren't defective! God didn't make a mistake when He made us! Of all the behaviors exhibited above, the good thing to recognize is that they are just behaviors, and behaviors can change. No matter how long you've exhibited them.

Let me explain further: I am a child of the '80s. I was raised on high fructose corn syrup. I love sugar. But as I've gotten older, I've seen how high sugar intake impacts my body. When I order coffee, I am adding all the syrups (and an extra pump or two), all the flavored creamers, some whipped cream on top, and then a few actual sugar packets for good measure. This has been me for three decades. In the last few weeks, I've been working on lessening my sugar intake. I've learned to adjust my taste buds to using less creamer and no sugar. I use Stevia. At first, I didn't think I could do it. I wanted to dump a half cup of sugar in my coffee like normal. After four weeks, I barely notice the difference, and I plan on keeping up with this going forward. Did I stop using sugar because I no longer liked the taste? No. I changed the behavior because while it was good going down, it wasn't good coming out. I changed the behavior because it no longer served the best part of me. Even though I had 30 years with this habit, I'm kicking it because I no longer want it to kick me. I'm not of the mind that people are 'set' and unchangeable. Do I believe it's harder the older you get? Yes. That's why you must get the fact that you can change in your head and heart. You may need to even repeat the following:

I AM A FINISHER?
I AM A FINISHER.
I AM A FINISHER!
Go ahead and say it. I'll wait.
No, I'm not, Candace.

Yes, you are! You've got to believe that. The book isn't titled *Letters to the Non-Finishers.* The book is titled *Letters to the Finishers (who struggle with finishing).* Not finishing is not who you are; it's just a behavior you exhibit!

Not finishing **is not who you are; it's just a behavior you exhibit!**

You might be thinking that this is some self-help mumbo jumbo. I can assure you that it is not. If you keep believing that not finishing is some type of deeply entrenched characteristic of who you are, you'll never get over it because you'll intrinsically believe you're not supposed to. You'll say what I used to say, "This is who I am." But, if you start to believe that you are in fact a finisher who just struggles with finishing, it's merely a behavior that you CAN change. The key to any kind of shift is changing the way you see yourself. You must change your mind about who you are and who you're not.

P.S. What are some behaviors you exhibit that you've embraced as irrevocable character traits? Make a list of them on one side. On the other, write out simple ways you can counter those behaviors.

2
Lazy Is Such a Strong Word

"Don't nothing work but work."
Zakia Blaine of @FBFBody

"Work, work, work, work, work, work, He said me haffi work, work,
work, work, work, work!"
Rihanna

Dear Finisher,

No one wants to be called lazy. It's harsh. It personally makes me squirm. When I hear it, I feel grossly inadequate. It feels like heavy layers of responsibility are being laid at my door. In fact, being called lazy impacts me in ways that other words don't. Sometimes, I have a physical reaction to the word. But, if I'm honest, in all my physical reactions, is getting to work one of them?

Rarely.

Listen here, Finisher. As a person who has exhibited lazy behavior, we need to just go on ahead and call a thing a thing. Lazy is defined as being unwilling to work or use energy. You want another adjective for it? How about slothful?

Indolent?

Shiftless?

Those don't sound too good, do they? Imagine someone calling you any number of these. Offended? That's valid. But we must ask ourselves why we are offended by these words but not by our own inaction. Here are a few more synonyms:

Lethargic.

Sluggish.

Slack.

Work-shy.

Negligent.

That last one? Whew!

I've often had to question how negligent I've been toward my own purpose. The truth is some of us haven't finished because we're avoiding the hard work it takes to do so. **We pursue ease, not effort.** We are not fond of the alternative set of words:

Hard work.

Sweat-equity.

Late nights.

Early mornings.

We are not interested in the consistent, tireless, plugging away at a goal without immediate gratification or results. I wasn't. Sometimes the most talented folks make the mistake of thinking that our gifts and talents create a path for us to walk without impediments. When our giftedness flows without difficulty, we start to believe that our journey should be the same. Believers, specifically, can start to believe that if God is with us, then we shouldn't have to work hard. But the Bible specifically says the opposite. From the beginning, even though God gave Adam the garden, He also set him in it to work it and take care of it. Proverbs 10:4 states, "Lazy hands make for poverty, but diligent hands bring wealth." Proverbs 14:23 states, "All hard work brings a profit, but mere talk leads only to poverty." Proverbs 20:4 states, "Sluggards do not plow in season; so at harvest time they look but find nothing." Then there's Proverbs 6:9-12, 2 Thessalonians 3:6-10, Proverbs 24:30-34, and Proverbs 12:11. The list goes on and on. Let's stop hiding behind God and our spirituality when we're…harsh word coming…just being lazy.

I've been in church most of my life, and sometimes, I've had the propensity to want to lean on God to do all the heavy lifting. There are many things I believe God promised me, but for the longest, I just sat around waiting for them to happen to me. People can speak blessings over our lives, but we have a part to play. And while we'll *say*, "Faith without works is dead," I'm not sure we live our lives in that truth. If a close relative who had a lot of money said to you, "You're going to be a multi-millionaire," how would you feel? Excited, right? I would be. But how would we walk out that promise in our lives? Some of us would go to work the next day and quit, talking about "My cousin said I'm going to be a millionaire!" Some of us would start spending the money before we even receive it. Why? Because we think that since our relative has the money, we're just going to be given those millions. But the close relative never said they were just handing over *their* multi-millions; they just made you a promise that you'd be one. They never said how you'd get there. What if how you got there was by managing the money you currently make better? What if it means you need to change your mind set about money? What if it means you'd have to give up having that $5 coffee you drink every morning? (That's almost $2,000 in savings a year right there). What if it means you have to downsize now to upgrade later? What if it means living below your means now so you could live at your means later? What if it means getting a second job at night so you could work on your God-dream during the day? What if it means actually working to have it and not just trying to look like you do? What if it means working 18+ hour days for a little while to make your dream come true? What if it means you cook all your food at home? What if it means getting over your imposter-syndrome (we'll discuss that later) to apply for jobs you think are out of your league? What if it means you find your identity in God and not what's currently on your back? What if it means you'll have to stop stunting for the 'gram? What if it means becoming more a giver so God knows he can trust you with more? What if it just means being obedient to what God is telling you to do?

Are you still excited?

God's promises aren't a passport to a life of do-nothingness or an excuse not to work hard. Constantly taking short-cuts around work only short-changes you and your intended result. Take it from me. Nothing will ever get produced without doing the work. Finishing takes work. You can delay it, but you can't deny it. At some point during the process, work will have to get done. Sure, I'm a gifted writer, but these letters weren't going to write themselves. No matter the level of giftedness, work must be put in. And work will not always be enjoyable. Work is hardly ever convenient.

Nothing is worse than being in the season of harvest but have nothing to gather because you never planted or plowed. Nothing is worse than a person trying to reap where they have not sown. If I'm honest, my reaping has been scattered because that's how I'd sown. I'd put a little work in here and a little bit there, but I never remained consistent. It wasn't the season that had me reaping sparingly; it was the way I had sown.

Why do we always want a 250% return on a 35% investment? Then we covet other people's harvest but not the work ethic that yielded those results.

I remember a time when I was leading a team, and one of the members started to get upset about some of the privileges of the leadership team. They wanted the privileges, too, and tried to guilt the leadership into believing they should get them. It almost worked. What I finally realized is that the leadership team and I weren't just reveling in undeserved favor; we earned the positions and thereby the rewards of those positions. We also had responsibilities that the other members did not. The complaining member didn't want to work hard. They didn't want to put in extra time when needed. They weren't interested in doing extra or above and beyond. Frankly, they weren't even doing the required amount for their position. They did the minimum but wanted all the perks of the hard work they were avoiding. They were sowing sparingly but wanting to reap bountifully.

We expect maximum output with minimal input. If we want to finish, we have to work. We can't cross the finish line reading books about running, going to conferences that teach the techniques of running, researching the best running shoes to purchase, or praying that God would give us "the spirit of running." All of that is wonderful. But eventually, we will have to put on those running shoes, put foot to pavement, and run!

"For just as the [human] body without the spirit is dead, so faith without works [of obedience] is also dead." James 2:26

Let's get to WORK, Finishers!

P.S. What are some tangible action steps you can take TODAY to finish? What are some ways that you've been 'waiting on God' when really, God is waiting on you? Write them down. Then make a commitment to do them.

3
A Finisher's PTSD

*"Be patient toward all that is unsolved in your heart and try to love
the questions themselves. . . . Live the questions now.
Perhaps you will gradually, without noticing it,
live along some distant day into the answer."*
Rainer Maria Rilke

"Why...Why? Tell them that it's human nature..."
Michael Jackson

Dear Finisher,

One of the best days along this journey toward finishing happened while I was having coffee with my mentor. First off, Dear Finisher, may I humbly suggest that you get one of those? A mentor. I think it's imperative. Not just anyone though. Get yourself a mentor (or three) who have walked the path you're currently on. Get someone who you can trust to call you to the carpet on your mess. Get someone who has your best interest at heart and doesn't just speak to your self-interest. Find someone who is still learning, too. Get someone who's kind to your tender heart but rough on your fleshly inclinations. Bottom line: Get a mentor. Ask God to send one. Seriously. What I know for sure is that God will send you what you need as opposed to what you want.

So one day, as I was having coffee with my mentor, I lamented my stop-start mentality and how I don't know how to get over it or even why it happens. She said something that was the catalyst for my change. She mentioned that while she was in her own therapy session (told you to get someone still on their own learning/healing path), she realized how much her own childhood trauma had more far-reaching impact on her current life than she originally thought. She wondered if that was also true for me. She challenged me to examine if my early-age sexual trauma had any impact on my ability to finish things.

"Sis, maybe your molestation is affecting you in ways that you haven't considered."

I stared back her blankly at first.

"Say what? What's being molested got to do with me not being able to finish things?"

"That's for you to answer."

She literally sips her coffee while staring at me over her glasses.

Can I just say she works my nerves?

Let me be honest with you: I really thought I was over that issue. I seriously thought I was past all the effects of the childhood trauma I incurred as a result of being molested. Sure, I had a few sketchy moments in my young adulthood, being triggered by certain touches or being awakened while sleep, but for the most part, I considered myself "normal." I was functioning like a well-adjusted human being. I'd gone to group and individual therapy as a kid. The perpetrator was removed from my life. I loved God, and I loved people. Wasn't I all right?

Maybe not.

I was so discombobulated by that entire conversation. I don't think I ever considered the emotional toll my trauma took on me. I always saw my trauma as contained within the boundaries of sex. It never occurred to me that trauma never stays contained; that it usually spills over your entire life. Remaking it. Remaking you.

When I left that meeting with her, I turned what she said to me over in my head multiple times. Of course, childhood trauma has long range impact for some people, but in this area? What did it have to do with finishing? I kept peeling back the layers of what my struggles really were. I looked at my behaviors and my whys. You know how a toddler goes through the "Why?" phase? I was just like that. I kept asking "But why?" I implore you, Finisher, to ask yourself "Why?" And don't be afraid of the answer.

"Why don't I finish?"

I just stop.

"Why do you 'just stop'? In what part of the process do you usually stop?"

Usually after the excitement of beginning something new wears off.

"So, after the starting line adrenaline is gone, what happens?"

I start filling my time with everything else, anything that's not what I'm supposed to finish.

"Like what? Name something."

Like, online videos or games on my phone. Something mindless that makes me feel good.

"Why? Why do you do this?"

. . . I'll get back to you.

Don't be afraid to face yourself. Sometimes, we're so busy pointing the finger outward, at all the things we believe hinder us *out there*, that we never take time to search within.

Some of us won't even be alone or quiet enough to hear what God might be saying to us. We're so afraid to face our own demons! So, we keep talking about the outside factors that won't allow us to succeed. It's always the other person—never you. To finish, we have to be able to really engage in truthful introspection. Get quiet and let God really tell you about yourself. Stop running from it. Stop only surrounding yourself with people who always agree with you. Do your inner work! Get down to the nitty-gritty. Crack open your past and figure out where some of your destructive behaviors come from. Go see a therapist, if need be. I promise it's worth it. On the other side of that digging is sweet freedom.

And finishing.

P.S. Something that helped me was starting a video diary. I record on my laptop. Record yourself asking yourself, "Why?" Sometimes truth can slip out of your mouth without you realizing it.

4
The Idol of Safety

"The dangers of life are infinite, and among them is safety."
Goethe

Dear Finisher,

As I shared in my last letter, I got to the bottom of my *whys*. Do you know what I found there? So much revelation!

First off, I have a great need to feel safe. I know — that's not terribly revelatory. Most who have had their safety stolen as a result of sexual abuse do. But, in an effort to create a safe environment around me, what manifested in me was the need for control and familiarity. I always needed a security blanket. I was scared to do anything that wasn't familiar. I had the same job for almost 15 years. Same place. Same people. Day in, day out. I liked what I did (for the most part), but I knew that God was calling me to something different, something unfamiliar. But because I knew this job well, I stayed. I stayed in a position that wasn't going any further and that no longer challenged me. But I knew the job. I was good at it. I was a leader in it. I knew what was expected of me. I didn't have to learn something new (and thereby possibly fail at it). I didn't have to be better or grow as a person. I was comfortable. I was safe. I would not leave. And so, because I would not crush the idol of safety in my life, God brought it down. Now I'm not saying that God shut the whole enterprise down for lil ole me...but it sure felt like it. Sometimes, in God's infinite grace, He'll make your disobedience walk away from you.

This need for safety was inhibiting my life in ways I could no longer afford. I wouldn't push past my comfort zones or enter any spaces—physical, emotional, or psychological—that were unfamiliar. Sometimes, we'll use God's hedge of protection to fence ourselves in. Every God-idea I ever had required a step of faith. God wanted me to become a water-walker. But I was paralyzed with fear in the boat.

Wait...lies! I wasn't in the boat. I was on the shore. Probably twenty to thirty feet away from the shore actually.

God sent someone a dream about me once. My friend said that she saw Jesus in the ocean with his arms outstretched. He was welcoming me. He was encouraging me to come to Him, to come out into the deep. There I was, on the shore, with my arms outstretched asking for Him to come to me. My friend then broke the dream down to me. She said that Jesus wanted me out in the deep with Him. He wasn't coming to get me from the shore. I was beckoning Him, and He was beckoning me. Her dream, those words, resonated with where I was in my life.

When I say I was paralyzed, I can't even begin to adequately explain how silently I tiptoed through my own life. No matter the amount of church shouts, trips to the altar, or sermons I preached, my behavior hadn't changed. I was clearly dealing with a stronghold, a place that has been fortified so as to protect itself against attack. And what I know about strongholds is we can't just shout a stronghold down. Even the children of Israel had to walk around the walls of Jericho first. But too many of us are avoiding the walk. We don't want to circle our issues. We just want the "shout," but that's not actually what's not going to bring the wall down. It's a part of the process for sure, but it's just the last step.

Wanting to be safe isn't a bad thing. Our human instincts are to keep ourselves safe. The problem is when we start making an idol out of being safe. God wanted to take me on an adventure, but I was resisting. Anything God calls us to do will require us to leave our comfort zones and trust Him on the journey. Most of time, you won't know what or where you're going. That's the point! We're not in control. And that's scary. Well, it scares me. Part of me "feeling safe" has to do with me being able to control my surroundings. That need for control gets in the way when God is trying to set us with new surroundings, with His new environment.

Control is an illusion. It's usually steeped in fear. Maybe it's fear of what will happen if we let go. We ask, *will we be hurt like before? Will we experience pain like we did that one time?* And here's the thing: we might. I'm not saying you'll experience trauma, but I would certainly be lying if I said we weren't going to experience pain on this journey. Trauma is painful. But every time you feel discomfort doesn't mean trauma is taking place. Stop equating the two. Whether we control everything and we perceive ourselves to be safe or we don't, we're still going to experience hurt. We should not want to spend all our lives trying to avoid pain that is essentially inevitable.

Successful childbirth and getting run over by a car both bring pain. One kills you and the other brings forth a miracle. Choose your pain. If I'm going to have to endure pain, I might as well get something out of it. If I'm going to endure pain, let it serve a purpose—God's purpose. His adventures will certainly bring discomfort. There will be heartache. But he also promised you peace. He also promised you His presence. He won't leave you when the going gets tough. He's going to be there. Finisher, you can trust Him with your life. Let me say it to myself: "Candace, you can trust God with your life. Relinquish your grip." Yes, that's it! I want the adventure more than the safety. It scares the hell out of me, but it simultaneously ushers heaven in.

P.S. What makes safety so appealing to us? Make a list of all the things you believe make you feel safe. Consider how this list is in conflict with the thing you are trying to finish.

5
Who Do I Run To?

Who can I run to? To share this empty space?
Who can I run to when I need love?
Xscape

Dear Finisher,

Once I realized I had a great need to be safe, I also realized what I would do when that safety was threatened or when I got overwhelmed. I'd escape. Remember, our minds are powerful. When I was being molested, my body went into protection mode. It would do whatever it had to do to keep me as safe as it could manage in a situation. Bessel Van der Kolk, in his book *The Body Keeps the Score* talks about this,

> Traumatized people chronically feel unsafe inside their bodies: The past is alive in the form of gnawing interior discomfort. Their bodies are constantly bombarded by visceral warning signs, and, in an attempt to control these processes, they often become expert at ignoring their gut feelings and in numbing awareness of what is played out inside. They learn to hide from their selves.

My body kept an excellent record of what to do with trauma, and my mind did the work of leaving. Where would she go? I don't know. I don't even remember. She'd just go away. Into my imagination. Back into dreamland, perhaps. She'd go wherever trauma wasn't happening. That became the way I functioned. Whenever I was faced with trauma of any kind, when anything would trigger my fear, anxiety, or worry, I'd retreat.

At one point, I wanted to start a T-shirt design company. I had pages filled with designs, quotes, and slogans. I'd get so excited because I just *knew* my designs would sell. And then, I'd start to think about where I'd get the T-shirt designed. *Which company was the best to print them? Should I go local or online? Where would I design them? On the drop-ship site or would I need design software? How much is design software anyway? I would need to trademark my designs and slogans. How do I do that? How much does that cost? What's the difference between trademark and copyright? I should take a class on that. Let me Google that. Uh, this seems complicated. Okay, let me go back and look at T-shirt print companies. Which type shirt should I pick? I want something soft, but those are more expensive. What should the name of my company be? Should I design a logo? Maybe I can do that now. Ugh! I would need that trademarked, too. Or would it need to be copywritten? I need someone who can help me work through this stuff because I'm confused. Let me Google that. How much? Ugh! Nevermind! This is too stressful!*

Enter my favorite YouTube clips. Or a Rom-Com movie. Or a favorite book I've read 20 times. Or games on phone.

This scene has played out countless times with so many projects that I'm low-key embarrassed to write this. But my truth is my truth. Whenever I'd get overwhelmed with any tasks, my mind would escape into comfort. Van der Kolk continues,

> Trauma, by definition, is unbearable and intolerable. Most rape victims, combat soldiers, and children who have been molested become so upset when they think about what they experienced that they try to push it out of their minds, trying to act as if nothing happened, and move on. It takes tremendous energy to keep functioning while carrying the memory of terror, and the shame of utter weakness and vulnerability.

For me, this often shows itself as distraction. I start something, and then I am *distracted* by YouTube clips, movies, group chats, cutting fruit, scrolling, or any other thing I just had to get done right then. It doesn't matter what it is as long it is something other than the task in front of me. Sometimes, I even use legitimate to-do list tasks to escape from the one thing I should be doing. This became easier to do when I got married. I've often used my role as a wife as a shield to hide behind when I didn't want to do what God was telling me to do. For example, my husband loves for me to cook for him. So sometimes, instead of writing, I'll cook dinner. Nevermind that he has agreed to cook for himself (which he does well, btw) because he knows I need to write and is fully supportive of me doing so. Or, I'll wash dishes. Or clean the bathroom (and I HATE to clean the bathroom). Now granted, I'm sure hubby appreciates all of that, but what he would appreciate even more is my finishing. Because he knows that it will fulfill my purpose, and he wants that more than a few chicken wings.

I told you before I stayed at a job far longer than I was supposed to in order to avoid purpose. I became a youth minister in order to avoid another call on my life. Finisher, don't hide behind all those roles. Some of us think if we just keep collecting roles, it will confuse God. Maybe it'll confuse all our friends and accountability partners, we think. Maybe, eventually, it'll confuse us.

It won't.

Once we're done escaping, the mission will still be there. It never leaves. I took a decades-long detour and yet here I am—back to where I started. Your mission never leaves. It only takes a deep breath and says, "Are you done?"

Here's what I learned about escaping: when I escape and come back to a task, I am usually a hundred times more stressed than when I left. Why? Because it's STILL NOT DONE! Escaping may have given me temporary relief, but it doesn't offer the real, soul-freeing relief of crossing it off my list, of finishing.

Face what is causing you to want to escape and deal with it. Once I did that, I realized that in order to deal with my habit of escaping, I needed to give myself "treats of escapism." I'll work hard for an hour or two, then I'll treat myself to 15 minutes of comfortable mindless activity. Yesterday, I realized I was having a rough day. You ever just wake up and know that productivity is going to be minimal? And sometimes, I'll push past it (we'll get into that in another letter). But sometimes, I discern that it's going to just be one of those days. I didn't work on the book. I knew I needed to. I had deadlines. But I was really struggling. So I treated myself. I let myself off the hook and did something else (productivity-wise). And today? I woke up early and went right back to writing. I feel refreshed after not laying my eyes on the page for 24 hours. I'm thinking straight, and the writing is flowing. If I go hard for a week or two, I'll take a day and do only what I want, which can include absolutely nothing. While writing this book, I've had days where I've gone to the library and worked for 6-10 hours straight. In celebration of my *go hard* writing day, I'd take off that evening. I'd watch a movie and relax. But, if I know I BS'd all day then that evening, it's writing and bed. If I finished a particularly daunting chapter, I'd treat myself to a night of scrolling and reposting memes. If it's a particularly rough writing day or week, I might have to treat myself hourly.

It looks like this: Congrats, Candace! You wrote for 45 minutes straight. Go into the group chat and see what's going on. Or play a game for 10 minutes. You finished two chapters today?! You deserve to start watching *Grey's Anatomy* from the first season for the millionth time! (stopping at Derek's death because...NO.)

And listen, you will have slipups. The closer I get to finishing, the more I feel like escaping! Don't punish yourself for the escape, curate it. You are not at its mercy; it's at yours!

P.S. Do you find yourself "escaping" when you should be working? What can you do to curate it instead of trying to eliminate the need altogether? Make a rewards list. When you finish a particular task, what's your reward? Print it and put it up in your work station.

6
My Complaining Addiction

*"If I would've known then, the things that I know now, I might not
have lost the time I complain about. Don't waste your time…"*
En Vogue

Dear Finisher,

I have an addiction. I was completely unaware of it until
hubby brought it to my attention. One day a few years ago, I
came home from work and started in on my usual course,
talking about my day. I was going OFF about whatever it was
that had happened that day. After about a half hour, he looked
up from his computer, took a deep heavy sigh, and said, "Did
anything good happen today? Does anything good happen ANY
day?"

I thought, *Does my husband want to die this day?* I couldn't be
sure.

As I furrowed my brows, ready to inquire about his health,
he added, "You complain a lot."

Oh yeah, he didn't want to live.

I suppose you can imagine what happened next. Yep, we got
into a full-blown argument! As can be my custom, I went petty.

"FINE! I won't tell you about my day any more. We don't have to talk at all! I'll just come in, cook you dinner, perform my wifely duties, and shut up since that's what you want!"

He stared back at me. "Really? All that?"

Yeah, I know I went too far. Too mas. But...

How dare he?! I don't complain a lot! When I got past my petty and listened to what he was saying, what I realized was I hardly ever see the glass full. Apparently, for me, it is almost always half-empty. And the wrong color. And it has a chip in it. And who washed these dishes? There are water spots all over them! Well no wonder! That isn't the correct sponge anyway. Ugh!

Welp.

I *do* complain a lot. Just saying that makes me want to cover my eyes in abject humiliation. This became even more real to me after I left my job (or it left me, which is one way to look at it). I was hanging out with some associates of mine. People were lamenting about their lives, including but not limited to relationships, jobs, money, church, etc. As I sat there, I realized that I had nothing to complain about. I didn't have anything upsetting to add to the conversation. Guess what I did! I started trying to search my brain for something, anything, to complain about. I wanted to be included! I wanted something to huff about! In that moment, I realized just how addictive complaining had become. When I would tell my husband about my day, it wasn't that something good hadn't happened all day. It was that I was laser-focused on the bad. That's what chronic complaining does. And frankly, if I exerted as much energy changing what I didn't like as I did complaining about it, maybe I'd have less to complain about.

Selah.

Some of us wouldn't know how to act if we didn't have something to complain about. I didn't. After being confronted by my husband, I took on a personal challenge to be more conscious of my complaining. I tried to look at the same scenarios I'd ordinarily complain about with "glass half-full" eyes. It wasn't easy. It's *not* easy. But you know what started happening? Once I stepped back from complaining, I started realizing how annoying it became to hear it from other people. Lord have mercy! Social media makes it even worse. The platforms are filled with people complaining about every and anything. It's exhausting.

Let me be clear: I'm not saying that we should walk around acting like terrible things aren't happening or that we shouldn't be able to vent about our feelings. But sometimes we use these platforms to complain about problems and yet won't sit down to finish the resolutions that God has dropped into our spirits. Maybe your finishing is the answer to the problems you keep complaining about. Going to work for me was so rough that I could not utter a kind word about anything or anybody there. I was sick of it all. We've all been there, right? In hindsight, the grace God had given me to deal with it had lifted. It was time to go and do what God was telling me to do. But no, I stayed and complained. I complained about people who I couldn't change, and I complained to people who couldn't do a single thing about my situation. And this is how you know you may be addicted to complaining. What's your prayer to complain ratio? If you spend 20 minutes complaining about something, how long do you spend praying about it?

Right.

If it's worth chronically complaining about, it should be worth your prayers. Because it's either time for absolution or time to be the solution.

P.S. Name two things you're currently complaining about. Write down specific ways you plan to change those issues. And if you can't see how to change the situation, maybe you're the one that needs to change.

7
You Good? You Good.

"I am the magic."
Myleik Teele

Dear Finisher,

I have this amazing ability to self-loathe to an almost pathological degree. I can rip myself apart in ways that my own worst enemy could not conjure.

You, too?

Yes, finishers seem to all have the same issues. We can pick ourselves apart and believe all the terrible stuff. For me, this usually happens after a bad day. If I wasn't productive, I would start in on myself and then it would quickly spiral into something else entirely.

Candace, why did you waste so much time today? You don't have time to waste time! This is a mess. You are a mess. You're a terrible human being. See? This is why we can't ever get anywhere! All you are is a professional quitter. You can't do anything right. People don't really like you. They only keep you around because they think they have to. You're not even friendly enough to have friends. You're a flat, slobby blob of a person. You dress terribly. Ugh. Look at those pictures. Look at your pimples. Look at the hair growing out of your face. People don't really like you. Folks don't really love you, not even your husband. I'm sure he thinks he made a mistake in marrying you. Just disgusting. You'll never progress. You'll never be better. You'll find a way to ruin it, to destroy it. Good things don't stick around you. You're not supposed to have a happy life. Wait. Something terrible will happen. Just you wait.

Writing that out makes me want to hurl. Do you see how fast it switched from me berating my behavior to beating me down? I would never (not even to my worst enemy) talk to or about someone like that. And I know God doesn't talk to me like that. So, who does that sound like?

That devil sings this song in the key of LIES.

Most of the future finishers I meet have some form of low self-esteem. We don't believe the good about ourselves. We actually refuse to believe it. We do, however, believe all the good stuff about others. Most of us can encourage, shout, clap someone else to their finish line while stoutly refusing to get to the starting line of our own.

How do you deal with compliments? Is your first inclination to explain them away? To tell the person giving out the compliment how wrong they are? What you believe about yourself is directly connected to what you believe you're capable of doing. I've found that the times I'm the least effective is when my esteem is in the toilet. I remember a time in my life when I felt left-behind, stupid, ugly, and worthless. I also remember that being the same time in my life when I was probably the least creative I have ever been. Connected? Yes, of course! God has infinite creative ability, and He's put something special in each of us as the crown jewel of His creation. But if we don't believe that, if we aren't able to see that special and good thing He's put in us, if we fail to see how worthy He makes us, what do we think we're going to do with His gifts? Nothing!

Once, I was so beaten down, so tired that I just couldn't utter a kind word to myself. My esteem was LOW. My husband (yes, the same one who tried it in the previous letter) was with me, hugging me, loving me as I sat at my kitchen table and cried about the mess that was me. Through a tear-streaked face, I lamented all the ways I sucked, all the ways I deemed myself unlovable and worthless. As he shook his head at me, ready to contradict every word I had prophesied over myself, he stopped. Instead, he recommended I write myself a letter of apology. He told me how hard I was being on myself and that I owed Candace (past, present, and future) an apology. He helped me upstairs to our room with one directive.

"Write and don't get up until you're done."

I sat for two hours and wrote. I apologized for all the ways I've treated myself, mistreated myself. I sobbed the entire time — not just because it was hard to do. I cried because it made me sad to see my mistreatment on paper, to see years of self-abuse in ink. Once I finished it, I resolved that I would do better by me. I would be a better friend to myself, and I would change my attitude about myself. I would reject the persona that the enemy was trying to force on me, and I would chase down God's original blueprint of who I am. I eventually published that letter to my blog because I thought it could help someone to know that how rough I can be with myself and that maybe they might need to write one, too.

You are not here by happenstance. God fashioned every single detail about you, bringing you into this world at this particular time. Whoever you are, whatever you have, whatever space you occupy, there isn't a mistake in it. Even the mistakes you've made are redeemable. You must believe these things, Finishers! It's torture trying to finish something while not believing in the power inside you to do so. That's how I spent most of my life—trying to succeed while concurrently not believing I could. I was a living example of what it means to be a house divided against itself. It can't stand. I have been a self-fulfilling prophecy my whole life in the opposite direction of my dreams.

I have to make a concerted effort to believe in my own magic. Previously, I mentioned imposter syndrome. It's a psychological pattern in which an individual doubts their accomplishments and has a persistent internalized fear of being exposed as a "fraud." Hear me. You know more than you believe you do. You have marketable skills—skills that others don't have. Tasks that come easy to you are supremely hard for others. You're not a fraud, I promise. I'm not telling you anything I haven't had to tell yourself.

I have a challenge for you. It's something I'm going to do myself. Write a list of 30 things that are good about you. Include things you do well, things you've accomplished, the things that makes you special. If you're struggling, call in friends/family/people you've worked with on projects/social media friends. Sometimes, other people will have a better (and clearer) view of who you are than you do. Every day for a month, read off something on that list. Read it aloud. Make yourself believe the good stuff about you. Seem strange? Maybe. But we don't have a problem telling ourselves how jacked up we are, right? So why is it so hard to even think about speaking life-giving words to ourselves? You are gifted. You belong in the room. You will finish. #BelieveThat

P.S. Two things this time. Make that list of 15-30 GOOD qualities you possess. Don't try to skip over this part. DO IT NOW. And then, write that letter of apology to yourself. You don't have to share it if you don't want. But write out the ways you've damaged yourself. If you need an example, go to my blog at ubu4him.com and look for "I'm sorry."

8
You Won't Feel Like It

"Now no feeling can be relied on to last in its full intensity, or even last at all. Knowledge can last, habits can last, but feelings come and go."
C.S. Lewis

Dear Finisher,

I'm writing this letter when I *really* don't want to be. My tonsils are swollen. I have a fierce sinus infection. And I have the cramps. All I want to do is curl back up in my bed and sleep some more. And who could blame me? I *am* sick, right? Those are the facts, but it isn't the truth. There's a difference. The truth is I'm not always going to feel like finishing. As I've mentioned before, there's certainly nothing wrong with taking breaks. Sicknesses happen. Life happens. There is nothing wrong with curling up in your bedspread and vegging out to an endless string of worthless movies. But sometimes we use life's inconveniences as excuses not to finish. There were times when I should have been writing when I didn't. Even when I was feeling a little better, I didn't write. If we're going to be the kind of finishers that finish, we're going to have to push through sometimes. We cannot allow our moods to rule and reign.

Yes, we have emotions for a reason, and we shouldn't ignore them. Emotions are God-given. However, as I heard John Piper say once, while our moods are great gauges, they can be terrible guides. Show up whether you feel like it or not.

Let me share something that might help us get this. About three weeks after I got married, I was laying atop my freshly made bed. Hubby and I had gotten into some weird disagreement (not even a *real* argument) about something. As I laid there, one tear slid out my eyes, then another. Before I knew it, I was in the throes of an all-consuming sob fest. I heard myself say out loud, "Oh my God, I shouldn't have gotten married! I made a mistake!" When I heard myself say it, it made me cry harder. I couldn't believe I felt like that after only three weeks of marriage! What was going on? Even through my tears, it felt like a really dramatic response to such a tiny disagreement. I ended up crawling beneath the covers and going to sleep.

When I woke up the next morning, I realized that my monthly menstrual cycle had come on. I legit laughed out loud in the bathroom. I wasn't falling out of love, I was PMS'ing. I no longer felt how I did yesterday. I went downstairs, kissed my husband, and thank God, went on with the marriage. Feelings are fleeting. They change. Usually, at the drop of a dime. I use that example only to illustrate that we shouldn't make permanent decisions in temporary mindsets. That's where our feelings often live (whether PMS-driven or not). Sometimes, we're going to have to suck it up and just DO what we must do even though we don't FEEL like doing it. If we only wait to feel like finishing, we'll never finish. Issues will always arise. Life happens. We cannot wait for only favorable conditions and feelings in order to finish. That isn't reality. Completion is *always* linked to commitment, and you know what commitment is? I do. I Googled it. It's defined as an engagement or obligation that restricts freedom of action. Commitment restricts freedom of action. Doesn't sound fun, does it? But it's the stuff finishing is made of. So even when I'm surrounded by balled up tissues, green juice, covers, and a heating pad, I'm writing. Commit to the decision you made to finish, and not the feeling you made it in.

P.S. What are three commitments you can make right now that you often don't complete because you don't "feel" like it?

9
Selective Amnesia

*"People have an annoying habit of remembering
things they shouldn't."*
Christopher Paolini

Dear Finisher,

Along with believing the good things you're capable of doing, you must learn to have a short memory for the mistakes you've made in the past. Selective amnesia will serve you well when trying to finish. Forget what happened before. I know it's not as easy as it sounds. Most of us have that *one* mistake that we can't get out of our thoughts. That *one* thing that defined (and really redefined) us. Mine is not completing college, not graduating. It was a serious blow to my esteem. On the report card of my life, there sits an "incomplete." I've tried to get back into school. One time, I even left my application on the desk of the admissions office and ran out! The admissions officer chased me down the street to give my application back to me. Can you imagine what that felt like? It's the one area of my life that brings me so much shame. It tells me that I'm not good enough, that I'll never be a finisher all because I didn't finish *that*.

But shame is a vision skewer. While yes, I didn't complete my degree, why do I allow that one experience with not finishing to completely invalidate all the things that I did finish? I opened this book with, "I hope I finish book." The assumption being that there's a possibility that I wouldn't. But the reality is I started and finished writing TWO stage plays in college that were produced and received rave reviews. In middle school—yes, middle school—I wrote a soap opera using my classmates as characters and passed out a chapter a week to keep people's interest. I've been writing creatively since I was a child. So why am I intimidated by a writing project when I've been successful in writing previously? Surely, if I've conquered writing before, I can do it again!

And that's just it! Forget what you *didn't* finish, and remember what you did!

I didn't finish the book I was working on to start (and finish) this one. So, you didn't finish your peas; you finished your carrots!

Finishers, we have to do something that, for most people, is incredibly hard to do—we must forgive ourselves. For too long, we've let our past have way too much say on our future. I've made mistakes. Small ones. And BIG ones. I've missed opportunities, went left when I should have gone right, and stayed when I should have left. I've hesitated when I should have advanced. I was quiet when I should have spoken up. Yet, every wrong turn I've made is and has been redeemable. The Bible says, "And we know that God causes everything to work together for the good of those who love God and are called according to his purpose for them" (Romans 8:28). Did you see that? *Those of us who love God and are called.* That verse should bring you comfort. Your mistakes were already accounted for. You can put all your shoulda coulda wouldas away! Those shoulda coulda wouldas will spin you into depression or worse if you focus on them. We have checks in the win column of life that we've forgotten! Focus on the wins, Finisher!

Here's the hardest thing to hear: TRY AGAIN.

Do you know how many projects/books I've started that laid somewhere in a drawer incomplete? TRY AGAIN.

Do you know that yesterday I didn't write anything? Like, nothing. And here I am. TRYING AGAIN.

Read that one more time: TRY AGAIN!

Oprah was told she was 'unfit for television.'

Walt Disney was fired from a newspaper where he worked citing his 'lack of imagination & good ideas.'

Stephen King threw out the manuscript for *Carrie* after it was rejected by 30 different book editors. His wife rescued it from the wastebasket.

Colonel Sanders was rumored to have been rejected by 1,000+ people before selling his franchise chicken idea and recipe. At 62.

Joseph had a dream that took several 'wrong' turns before it came true.

Remember the losses but only to recall how far you've come. Most importantly, remember the wins to bolster you for the journey ahead! It's going to work this time. TRY AGAIN! We've won before, and we will win again!

P.S. What is one area of life where you need to try again? Write about that area, why you're scared to and then put together a specific plan for tackling that issue again.

10
Accountability Matters

Dear Finisher,

I'm writing this letter because my accountability partner (my husband) checked in on me about my writing. His nudge made me think of something that we finishers need to remember. Too often, we don't like for people to know what we're trying to finish because we don't want someone breathing down our necks. We don't want someone reminding us every day that we need to push toward our goal. It's easier to have an off day when no one knows about it.

Or is it?

The fact is, finishers who struggle to finish *need* accountability. We need someone (or a group of someones) who can check in with us and make sure we're doing our work. Accountability partners make sure we're taking consistent steps toward our goals. Is it always fun? No. Will it expose you? Yes. But it's a necessary part of our journey. The only reason this letter exists is because accountability dug into my behind.

Every day, he asks, "How's your book coming?"

"How much did you write today?"

"How's it going?"

On the days I have something good to report, I love it. But on the days when writer's block has crept in or when I've spent most of the day watching clips online, it's annoying. And guess which days I mostly have? You got it. The distracted ones. I wouldn't be a finisher without them. And it feels like (even though I know this isn't the case) all the inquiries into my productivity are attacks. But here's the truth: Accountability is not an attack. Realize that anyone who dares to check in on our productivity isn't trying to hurt us. Their goal is the same as ours, a finished product. They want us to "see Z" as badly as we do. But they know (and we know) that we can't "see Z" without consistency in running through the rest of the alphabet.

Support isn't just hand-holding. Support isn't just rubbing your back, giving you money, or giving you hugs to make you feel better. Support isn't one-dimensional in that way. Sometimes support is kicking you in your ass, calling out lazy behavior, questioning your methods, or telling you that you're full of crap.

Finisher, get an accountability partner or several. It's imperative that it be someone we can't manipulate. We creatives have PhDs in manipulation. We do it well. We cry, blame-shift, and make excuses better than anyone else. But we also need to answer to someone. And honestly, it should be someone who doesn't think like you. Someone who doesn't look at life through your lens. It should be someone who loves you enough to tell you the truth. Someone who can call you to the carpet and who isn't moved by your tears or excuses. I have a husband (I see him daily), a writing group (we meet online weekly), a writing mentor (I see her monthly), and people who, usually on the unction of the Holy Spirit, get at me (usually when I'm most distracted). We have all the same goal—me finishing. Inspiration isn't what pushed me to write this letter to you. It was accountability. It wasn't warm. It wasn't fuzzy. But it got the job done.

And let us consider how we may spur one another on toward love and good deeds - Hebrews 10:24

P.S. Who are your accountability partners? If you don't have any, why is that? This week, reach out to two people who could serve in that capacity.

II
EFF the I.S.

"For a man to conquer himself is the first and noblest of all victories."
Plato

Dear Finisher,

I have a word of advice for both of us. It's something that becomes harder the closer you get to your goal. You *must* ignore your inner saboteur. I call it the I.S. This is possibly one of the hardest lessons I've had to learn. The I.S. tells you that you have plenty of time to finish, there's no need to rush. The I.S. tells you that your work is obsolete. It says that no one needs this project you've been toiling over for months or even years. Your I.S. specifically tells you that whatever revelations you've had about this project have been said or done already. It convinces you that you have nothing of worth to add. Your I.S. tells you that it's too late to begin again, tells you you're too old to keep at it. It says you're not who you know you are.

Your I.S. will also pick the wrong projects, projects that are impossible for you to win in. And you won't win not because you aren't capable. You won't win because they aren't yours to win. Sometimes, we pick projects or people who we aren't supposed to engage or conquer. And then when it falls apart, it feeds the narrative that we aren't worth anything. If a fish can't climb trees, does that mean it's been an unsuccessful fish? No. It means that trees are the wrong environment for them to flourish in. Now that metaphor may seem sophomoric, but how many of us do that? We fish keep looking at the squirrel's success at climbing trees, wanting to do what they can, and steadily becoming unhappy with our own unique abilities. We buck against the ecosystems God has set up for us. Then what do we do? We jump out of the water, flop on the shore, and try to do what the squirrel is doing. We deprive ourselves of the air WE need (water) and kill ourselves in the process. How many of us are killing ourselves trying to keep pace or keep up with something that was never meant for us in the first place?

I remember when I first became a minister. I wanted so badly to fit in. I wanted everyone to like me. I wanted to look/act like everyone else. I'd been doing that my whole life. So there I was, joining a ministerial staff wanting to be everyone but myself, wanting to blend in so badly that I sabotaged any uniqueness that dared come up. I dressed like everyone else. I tried to preach like everyone else. I wanted all my messages to sound like everyone else. One day, we were having a youth event, and the preacher for that event got sick at the last minute, and I had to go up instead. I was so scared. I didn't have anything prepared! I was wearing jeans, a white tank top, and crop top denim jacket—not my suit or even the customary Christian T-shirt. I didn't have time to overthink it or let the I.S. have its way. I got up there, and I was authentically me. I used object lessons (love them!) and just sounded like I was having a regular conversation. It was probably one of the best sermons I've ever preached to date. The I.S. isn't just about making you fail. The inner saboteur also works by making you try to succeed as your false self. Because listen, if you ain't winning authentically, you ain't winning at all.

Your I.S. also loves to compare. It loves to scroll Instagram and look at people's perfectly curated pictures and remind us of how imperfect we are (more on that later). Your I.S. will remind you of the truth of your deficiencies but never remind you of the tools in your possession to overcome them.

Bottom line? Your I.S. is your enemy. Do not entertain it. It will use a little truth to float a larger lie. The larger lie is simple: We can't. No matter how the I.S. packages it, Finisher, it's still the same lie. But the truth is we can! The only card that trumps *can't* isn't *can*, it's DO. The only way you'll know you *can* is when you do it. When you start doing, you'll look back and be astounded that what your I.S. told you was an impossibility is now complete.

You belong to your father, the devil, and you want to carry out your father's desires. He was a murderer from the beginning, not holding to the truth, for there is no truth in him. When he lies, he speaks his native language, for he is a liar and the father of lies. - John 8:44

The thief comes only to steal and kill and destroy; I have come that they may have life, and have it to the full. - John 10:10

P.S. How does your inner saboteur show up in your life? Name at least three ways you see it at work and three ways you can shut it up!

12
Busyness is not the Business!

"Beware the barrenness of a busy life."
Socrates

Dear Finisher,

Handle your busy-ness so you can handle your business. Some of us don't struggle with the finish line because we're just laying around being lazy all the time. Some of us are filling our lives with new projects, projects that bring excitement and won't remind of us of the ones we haven't completed. We will pick up a new hobby, meet up with friends, host gatherings for other creatives, shop, wash dishes, start other creative projects, pick up extra work, get another church position (I SAID WHAT I SAID), get married (I SAID WHAT I SAID), have a baby (I SAID WHAT I SAID), get another degree (I SAID WHAT I SAID), and the list goes on and on. None of these things are wrong in and of themselves. However, if we're using any of the above (or anything else on your list of busy-ness) to distract us from finishing what we started, then it's a problem. A) It won't work. Purpose is a relentless huntress. B) How dare you use these very good things and turn them into mere interruptions? C) If you're using marriage or children to run from purpose, you're not only harming yourself, but you're adding folks to your body count. It is irresponsible and cruel to drag other people into our nonsense. When we take other paths that aren't included in God's plan, we can hold up more than just our lives; we can impact others.

Let me be clear: even our detours are redeemable. That said, redemption isn't insulation from consequences. Look at the biblical Jonah. Out here just being totally disobedient and jacking up others in the process. God told him what he needed to do and where he needed to do it — go preach to the city of Nineveh. Jonah refused. He not only refused, but he went in the opposite direction. He boarded a ship to Tarshish. While he was on the ship, a great storm arose and was about to capsize it, probably killing everyone on board. Meanwhile, Jonah is asleep.

Here these men are, sailing along on their journey, and they're about to go down on account of someone else's tomfoolery. And said fool is asleep – totally unaware of the havoc his disobedience has wrought. These men had no idea when they met Jonah that he was on the run (from God). They might have thought Jonah was on a business trip. Nope! Jonah was on a busy-ness trip, avoiding the business he was supposed to be taking care of.

Sound familiar?

We've got to do better. Busy-ness is often the only culturally accepted opioid. We'll use anything to not have to think and to not have to feel that feeling we hate to feel — failure. So we pick up extra shifts of busy-ness while our business falls by the wayside. Avoidance (called by any and many other names) is still avoidance.

And what happens when we get bored with these other "projects?" Our business, our God-idea, will still be there. You can't outrun it. It's too high to get over and too low to get under!

(Thanks, Michael!) No matter how much busy-ness you throw at your business, it will still be there. It's not going to go away. Purpose is a relentless huntress *and* a clingy boyfriend! No matter how many times you try to shake it, purpose will never truly let you go. And here's the awesome thing: you don't want it to. Your sweet spot isn't in the quantity of projects, it's in the quality. If my 24 hours are filled to capacity, but I still haven't scratched the surface of purpose, I've been wasteful with this life. I don't care if I finish every single thing on my laundry list of to-dos, if I don't finish what's on God's to-do list for me, what have I really accomplished? Finisher, get clear on business vs. busy-ness because only one has a finish line worth crossing.

P.S. Create two columns. On one side put business and on the other busy-ness. Think about every project/job/major task in your life. What are you filling your life with and why?

13
Give Your Good Gifts!

"To avoid criticism, do nothing, say nothing, and be nothing."
Elbert Hubbard

Dear Finisher,

Today, a friend of mine came to a personal revelation about themselves, and I was instantly frustrated. Not with her, but with myself. I often don't say what I'm thinking or feeling, especially as it pertains to others. What does her revelation have to do with me? Well, that revelation was one she could have possibly had at least two to three years prior if I had just opened my mouth.

Finisher, why don't we think that our contributions to the world are worth it? We keep our gifts clutched in our hands, close to our chest, afraid that what we offer the world isn't good, won't be accepted, and isn't somehow enough! Why do we think so little of our God-given gifts and potential that we won't just let them go? Here's one reason why: we start from the wrong space. We're starting with ourselves. We are starting with how we feel about what's inside of us. That's where we got it twisted. You don't lay ownership to what you offer to the world; you are simply the conduit through which it passes. If it's not good and enough, then what you're really saying is the God who gave it to you must not be either. Whether it's accepted by anyone else or not, well, that's not up to you. I am often in my head so much about whether something will be received. Hear me: That's (clap) NOT (clap) YOUR (clap) JOB! (clap). Your job is to put it out in the world and let the chips fall where they may. Get out of your head and out of your own way.

Some of us aren't finishing because we're scared to submit our offering to the world. We are fearful of what our finished work looks like to those around us. If we can keep "working on it," then we never have to suffer the inevitable opinions and critique.

Chile. Sometimes I won't circulate a true or hilarious meme because of a misspelling or a grammar mistake. I remember one time, cracking up at this video and I wouldn't share it because I caught a few grammar issues. That seems silly, right? But the thing is that kind of thinking permeates my entire being and creative offerings. How often don't I share because of imperfections? It takes me way too long to finish blogs because I'm always double-checking everything I write, over-thinking it, and frankly, over-explaining myself, worried that what I say will be taken the wrong way in this hyper-sensitive, cancel-culture. Frankly, it's exhausting. But what I'm doing is putting the person who may critique my work ahead of the person who may need my work — even if that person is me. Even as I write these letters, I'm trying constantly not to edit myself. If I'm honest, it's because I'm scared of what the theologians, the pontificators, and the critics will say. But you, Finisher, may need to hear/read what I'm saying. So now I'm going to hold up me *and you?*

Know this — whatever you offer to the world, it won't be perfect. If you're waiting for it to be, you'll never put it out. There will always be something to criticize. Truthfully, even if it *was* perfect, someone would still criticize it. That's what they do.

Consider that maybe our need to wait until something is perfect has more to do with how we feel about ourselves rather than the project. Deep down, do you feel imperfect? And if you can't control and fix everything single thing about yourself, you'll work hard to fix it in what you do. Maybe what you're ultimately trying to fix is you. What you're afraid to have criticized isn't just your work — it's you.

Take your idea/project/assignment/purpose out of the shadows. Do your best (not your perfect) work. Exert the effort. Don't be languid about it. Expect critics and finish it anyway. (See Matthew 25:14-30 MSG for an amazing story about offerings, unearthing your talent and why perfection is indeed the enemy of progress.)

P.S. After reading the above scripture, think about one thing you currently have "buried" out of fear of criticism or backlash. Maybe it's a God-idea. Maybe it's a decision you're scared to pull the trigger on. Put it at the top of a piece of paper and the worst-case scenario of that decision at the bottom. In between, make a pro/con list. Examine whether most of your cons are centered around people's opinions. What does that tell you about your next steps?

14
Gather Your Helps

"...small support could accomplish a big dream"
Mohammad Rishad Sakhi

Dear Finisher,

Gather your helps!

Yes, I know that sounds weird. If you're a finisher (who struggles to finish), you know that most of the time, you don't feel like doing your work. We've already talked about that. So, when those moments come (and they will), you must gather the helps! What's your #finishingforeplay? What puts you in the mood to finish? As I'm writing this chapter, I am sitting in the middle of my made bed, leaning back on my reading pillow, candles lit, and the *Hamilton* soundtrack playing in the background. I had my spinach smoothie this morning (which gives me a burst of energy and keeps me full without the typical sleepy effects of a heavy breakfast), read my devotional, and had some good Jesus time. I opened up my group chat online for a giggle when I needed a mental break and read what I wrote the previous day to get inspired for what I need to do today.

I keep my snack of choice (Craisins), vision board, and inspirational quotes handy because eventually I will need them. Aesthetics matter to me. My laptop and external hard drive match. I live for colorful pens and sticky notes, my notebooks are inspirational, and my folders are pretty. It all matters to me! My work bags are pretty and super functional. I often hold work dates where I'll get with a fellow creative, writer, or entrepreneur, and we'll knock our to-do lists out together. Sometimes, you need a partner to be inspired with. This and more puts me in the mood to finish.

I know. I do the most. Sometimes *too* much.

I'm not saying you need all of this extra-extra to finish, but I am saying that everybody needs help. What that looks like for you can be (and will be) very different from mine. Find your joy in finishing! What makes you *want* to finish? What environments work best for your optimal creative energy to flourish? Do you need complete quiet? Are mornings best for you? (they are for me). Do evenings work better after you've put the kids down? Maybe lunchtime at your 9-5 is optimal? Maybe weekends? Do you have a favorite spot in your house? Maybe a well-worn chair? Is there a playlist that gets the juices flowing? Do you create better after a workout? I mean, that's not my testimony, but maybe it's yours!

I believe we all have a creative rhythm, and figuring out what works for you can really aid you in finishing. For instance, I tend to organize my areas before I start something new. It's hard for me to think straight with mess in my eyeline. Those dishes downstairs though? Not in my eyeline; doesn't bother me. What are your proclivities? I know my friends probably judge my pen obsession. Let them! I shall not be put to shame! Lebron James has routines and processes that aid him in his greatness. Why shouldn't I have some? (Did I just compare myself to King James?) The point is, figure out what your rhythm is and what helps inspire you.

P.S. Start to clock when you feel your most creative and start a list of your "helps." Try to gather as many as you can when it's time for you to finish.

15
It Goes Down in the "D"

"Discipline is the refining fire by which talent becomes ability."
Roy L. Smith

Dear Finisher,

So now that I've given you full freedom to air out all your crazy with your tools for "foreplay," we should talk about what we don't want to talk about. What happens when your favorite spot in the house is covered with your child's art project? What happens when your favorite pen busts all over your pretty work bag? You didn't get your pre-creating workout in, your playlist isn't working, and there is no silence to be had in your whole house. What then? It's often seen as a dirty word to the finishers who struggle to finish. We don't think we possess this attribute. We think this word is reserved for the go-getters, the ones who don't need these letters. But it's not true. We, too, can have possession of the word. So here's it is. Try not to cringe when you read it.

DISCIPLINE.

I know, I know. That nasty, unattainable word.

There's good news and bad news about discipline. The good news is that discipline isn't unattainable. We all have it. And I know what you're thinking. You're saying, "No, I don't, Candace!" Yes, you do. Everyone has a measure of discipline;

you just have to learn that those skills are transferable. Discipline is simply training ourselves to do something in a controlled and habitual way. If you've ever gotten up every day at a certain time, you've got discipline. If you've ever done a task that is ultimately good (or even bad) for you for several days or weeks in a row, you've got discipline. I used to believe the lie that discipline is something that certain people have and others don't. I used to think that I didn't have discipline. I don't believe that anymore. I have it. I just choose not to employ it as often as I should.

I went on a 12-day smoothie detox. Nothing but smoothies, fruits, and vegetables for 12 days. If you knew me, you'd know what a major feat that was. I live for every sweet, every block of cheese, and every butter and bread product made. I now make my bed almost every day (whether I'm working from home or not). I never used to make my bed. (I never saw the point of it all.) All I'm saying is discipline can be learned.

Here's the bad news, Finisher. Discipline has nothing to do with your feelings. We finishers rely heavily on our feelings. It's where our creative whimsy lies. You ever have that sensation where you're bursting with creative finishing ju-ju, seemingly unable to wait until you get to do whatever it is you do? For me, it's usually right after a shower. I get my best ideas in the bathroom. After a great shower, I can't wait to get dressed and let my fingers fly across the keyboard. That's inspiration. Everything I talked about in the previous letter about your #finishingforeplay (what gets you in the mood to finish)? That's to aid in inspiration. But discipline? Discipline is less inspiration and more perspiration. Discipline comes in when you have absolutely no ju-ju. It comes when there are no more bathroom revelations, or when you feel like crap and perhaps haven't gotten out of the bed in several days. Discipline doesn't care about your moods, your playlists, or your pens. Discipline shows up when inspiration leaves, as she's prone to do. She's a fickle creature. Inspiration loves to start, but discipline is what will get you to finish.

Here's the secret that no one will tell you: perspiration can often lead to inspiration. Sometimes, we creatives think it works the other way. Nah. Don't believe it. Discipline has often dragged me, kicking and screaming, to my creative whimsy.

For example, as I'm writing this, I'm not having a good day. I'm sad and a bit overwhelmed. I haven't showered, my hair is a hornet's nest, my bed isn't made, and I haven't left it for more than an hour at a time in days. I don't care about those pretty pens I mentioned before, the folders, or my snacks. There isn't any inspiration I can access. But there *is* discipline. Discipline is not my enemy, nor is it yours. On my bad days, she is my friend. Discipline nudges me out of my flattened space in the mattress and urges me on. She makes me take a shower and open my laptop. Discipline makes me put one finger on the keyboard until sentences flow out. Discipline helps me get it done. She is helping me get it done as we speak. She couldn't, however, convince me to wash my hair though. She's powerful, but she's not Jesus.

P.S. Based off the definition of discipline, what are some areas in your life where you're currently applying discipline? How can you transfer that skill over to that project you're trying to finish?

16
Taking the Easy Way Out

"The easy way out usually leads back in."
Peter Senge

Dear Finisher,

I need to be honest with you. I've spent over a year at home just writing. I wasn't working, sometimes not even part-time. I am grateful for that time because it's a privilege that not many artists can experience. But it was also was very difficult for me. I've had a job since I was 15 years old. I don't think I realized how hard it would be to stop working and start purposing. Not making my own money (ultimately feeling like I wasn't pulling my weight for my family) has driven me to distraction on many days. Even though I sincerely felt I was on God's path, even though I was fortunate enough to have a partner who supported my decision to solely write, it was wearing on me. I wanted money. My own money. I wanted my back account to look like it did when I was working a full-time job. So recently, I applied for a job that I knew I could get. I was tired of not having money readily available. Having a job would be the path of least resistance for me, *the easy way out.*

71

If I got that job, then I would have the money I so craved. But it would also give me an out. I could blame lack of time or focus on why I couldn't finish this book. That's the path I've always taken, and it hasn't gotten me any closer to finishing. Don't get me wrong! There's this rumor going around that having a paying 9-5 job is the death of all things creative and entrepreneurial. That's a lie. Don't let anyone have you believe that foolishness. But for me? Right now? God needed me to be singularly-focused. And in His great-providence, He allowed my home situation to be such that I could be (Thank you, Lord!). God was no longer allowing me any room to be disobedient. He legit forced me out of a job that He'd been asking me nicely to leave for years. He allowed every financial well to dry up. You know why? Because if I'm going to be financially viable, He's going to make it come from my own hand (and His). That may not be your story. But consider what your path of least resistance is. What's your easy way out? We all have one. It's the path we veer onto when the current path is rocky. When the current one isn't giving us immediate gratification or granting us quick access to what we want. When the path we're on is stretching and molding and showing us who we really are, we leave it. We move to a path that makes us feel good and right and in control. But there's no finishing over there. That path only leads us away from what we ultimately want.

And here's the thing. There are multiple paths that will take you off course. They will be varied and different but always with the same end — unfinished purpose. Sure, everyone's story isn't one of purpose dragging us up the rough side of the mountain. But we finishers (who struggle to finish) often look for the easy exits on the highway of life, and that is never how you get to your destination. Easy is not *always* going to be your portion, and it's certainly not going to be where you finish.

P.S. In what ways are you currently taking the easy way out? How is that showing up in your life? Write out one step you can take toward your purpose that you haven't taken for fear of it being 'hard.'

17
Sacrifice

"I think that the good and the great are only separated by the willingness to sacrifice."
Kareem Abdul-Jabbar

Dear Finisher,

What are you willing to sacrifice to see 'Z'? It's a question I've had to ask of myself multiple times. And sometimes, I'll say things like "whatever it takes," but then wonder if I really mean that. Sacrifice means the destruction or surrender of something for the sake of something else. Destruction or surrender. What are you willing to destroy or surrender for the sake of finishing? If I'm honest, at first, the answer was nothing. I didn't want to lose anything or surrender much to get to this finish line. I wanted my life to continue along in the same way it had been. I wanted to remain the same. I'd decided that I would just fit finishing in when or *if* I could. I wanted to remain on the corner of ease and comfort. But ease and comfort wouldn't get me to my destination, and it won't get you to yours either. I had to make finishing my priority, not an after-thought. To do that, I had to start sacrificing. It started with my time.

My time is my own. As an only child and having been single for many years, my personal time has been my highest valued commodity. But finishing commandeered my time in a myriad of ways. Personal time that could have been used doing whatever it is I wanted to do had to be put toward finishing. Sometimes, it required me to be up late, tapping away on my laptop when everyone else in my home was sleep. Late nights. Early mornings. Sometimes, it meant I couldn't hang out with friends because I was chained to my desk. I wanted my weekends to remain off-limits for work, and that wasn't always possible. Some Saturdays saw me looking out the window wistfully while I sat on my couch surrounded by notebooks. I couldn't afford to attend certain events because this 'purpose-driven entrepreneurial/creative life' doesn't always yield immediate monetary dividends.

Can I get a witness?

See, purpose doesn't always care about what you *want* to do for the moment. It cares only about what you said you wanted to do to impact eternity. I had to learn to relinquish the reliable, methodical cadence of my own life. I had to be willing to be disrupted. Temporary inconvenience for permanent improvement. That's been (and continues to be) my mantra. And make no mistake, it's not easy to live it day in and day out. The sacrifices we may be willing to make to cross our finish line might mean disappointing those closest to us. You may not be able financially contribute as you would have before. Your availability may be limited. Everyone won't get it, and frankly, they don't have to. It's not their finish line; it's yours.

I've had to sacrifice pride and my ego during this time. It's been beyond difficult. It's been open-heart surgery while I'm awake. I couldn't do what I normally would have done. The way I show love is often through gift giving. Right now, that isn't possible. The lack of funds is real. Not just because I'm not currently working, but because any funds that I do get are earmarked for my finish line. Projects and purpose cost money! Marketing, makeup, travel, business cards, website design, etc.! I was somewhat prepared for that, but what I didn't anticipate was the guilt that accompanied it. I felt like I was letting everyone down, and truthfully, I felt less-than because I couldn't do what I normally would. Not only that, but instead of pouring out, I had to let folks pour into me. Something as simple as friends paying for movies became such an ego-crush. I didn't like the feeling of folks taking care of me and me not being able to pay them back. When I say open-heart surgery, I mean that! No anesthesia! I remember getting into an argument with a close friend because she kept inviting me out and paying for me. Movies. Coffee. Dinner. How dare she?! We kept going back and forth about it for months. Me feeling guilty and her rolling her eyes and telling me to "hush up and say thank you." Finally, she said to me "Candace, I would hope our years-long friendship is deeper than a few dollars."

Well then. That succinctly ended that.

Sacrifice what you must, Finisher, but don't be a martyr when you don't need to be. You can sacrifice without being in a perpetual state of suffering. I thought the two were synonymous. They are not. There will absolutely not be any finishing without sacrifices, but please destroy and surrender properly.

P.S. What is one thing you've been reluctant to sacrifice in order to make it to your finish line? Write or type out the quote "Temporary Inconvenience for Permanent Improvement." Write your sacrifice under temporary inconvenience and your end goal/finish line under permanent improvement. Keep it some place where you can see it every day.

18
Eat the Elephant Every Day

"Just take the stab/Just take the swing/Just take the bite/Just go all in"
A Perfect Circle

Dear Finisher,

Finishing is not a one-time commitment. Finishing is a daily decision. It's an hourly choice. It's a minute-by-minute resolve and a by-the-seconds determination. I used to think that if I decided on a Monday to finish, that decision should carry me through until the end. And maybe for some people, it works that way. But for me and my house? I have to decide to finish every day, over and over and over again. I have to decide when I wake up in the morning to finish. I have to decide after I eat breakfast to finish. I have to decide when I open my laptop to finish. I have to decide when I look at the remote control to finish. I have to decide again when I want to lay in the bed all day. My decision manifests as me getting up and going to a local coffee shop to get work done. THAT is what finishing looks like to those of us who struggle with it. We have to decide and then keep deciding that our answer will be yes.

I hate that.

It's exhausting to keep deciding. But isn't that what marriage should look like? Sure, I made that one grand declaration at the church that one-time. It was great! But my marriage is sustained by 2,000 tiny decisions we make every day. When I choose to put the toothpaste back where I got it because I know it bothers him when I don't. When I apologize rather than hold on to my pride. When I accept his apology even though I'd rather stay mad 'cause it feels good to just sit in my epic-rightness. When I give him the bigger two pieces of corn on the cob even when he KNOWS I love corn more than him! Okay, wait a minute. Let me take a deep breath. I think I slipped into something else! I'm just saying. We must keep deciding.

Deciding is a push when I wanted a glide.

Most of us aren't going to glide to the finish. If that were the case, we'd be there already. Every day, you have to walk in your decision to finish. You decide and then walk that decision out. You eat the elephant.

What, Candace?

It's a riddle.

How do you eat an elephant?

One bite at a time.

I get so overwhelmed with how massive a goal is that ten minutes into starting, I'm ready to give up. The end doesn't seem anywhere in sight. Fifty years of matrimony may seem like an insurmountable goal. But getting through June may not. Or maybe just getting through this day.

Finisher, a word of advice: don't look at that elephant as a whole. It will stress you out. It's too much. Too big. Just pick up a fork and a knife and start eating that elephant's foot. Move up to the leg. Eat all four of those legs. Start in on the belly. Before you know it, you'll be eating the ears and carving up the tusk.

After a while, you'll look up and realize the whole elephant is gone. You ate it.

I didn't just *arrive* at Letter 18. I had to start with Letter 1.

Finisher, write the sentence instead of worrying about the whole book. Don't concern yourself with filling the whole canvas, start with one brush stroke. Post on social media TODAY instead of thinking about curating the perfect IG feed. Losing 20 pounds feels insurmountable? Drink only water this week. Take the stairs instead of the escalator next week.

If the finish line looks too far away to think about, just put one foot down. And then another. Just worry about the next step.

Eat the elephant, y'all.

One bite at a time. One. Bite. At. A. Time.

P.S. Are there any goals you can break up into smaller goals? For instance, instead of being overwhelmed at having to hit a huge word count, I broke it up into a daily and hourly word count. How many words would I need to write if I wrote for two hours a day? What does this look like for you? Write out three small easy steps you can take toward a big goal. Once you complete those steps, do it again. Continue until complete.

19
Redefine the Unknown

"One is never afraid of the unknown; one is afraid of the known coming to an end."
Krishnamurti

Dear Finisher,

I am anxious. Quite a bit. Finishing had caused me major anxiety. Sometimes, it's the anxiety of starting. Sometimes, it's the anxiety of looking at a blank page and knowing I have to fill it. (I know, y'all. I'm eating the elephant. I promise!) There's also the anxiousness that comes with thinking that what I write is stupid. Even anxiety that *I'm* stupid. But ultimately, my anxiety stems from the fact that this enterprise is completely unknown territory. Sure, I write. I have a blog. I've already mentioned all my previous writing experiences. But this? This is different. I have no idea what will come of this book. I mean, I have the audacity to give advice? *Am I crazy?*

Maybe a little. You've got to be slightly mad to finish. But lately, there's been this other nagging anxiety. It's the anxiety of the undone. What happens if, as I keep aging, I don't ever tap into all my potential? What if I leave this world with it all undone? I remember actress Viola Davis said something in her Oscar acceptance speech that rocked me to my core. She said,

> *"You know, there's one place that all the people with the greatest potential are gathered. One place and that's the graveyard. People ask me all the time, what kind of stories do you want to tell, Viola? And I say, exhume those bodies. Exhume those stories. The stories of the people who dreamed big and never saw those dreams to fruition..."*

I don't want to be one of those whose story must be told by someone else because I didn't have the cojones to tell it myself. I don't want to be where potential gathers. I want to be where potential was exhausted. I want to dream big and accomplish bigger. The anxiety of undone is usurping the anxiety of unknown. Unknown is really an illusion. The unknown has been wrongly perceived by your senses if all you feel in response is anxiety. Consider this: when you go on vacation to a place you haven't yet been, does it cause you anxiety? Do you think *I'm not good enough for Maui. London is too good for me. Japan is beyond my reach*? Of course not! That sounds ludicrous! You're excited for a new adventure to experience and explore. Why then do you talk yourself into fearing this particular unknown? Both scenarios require you to encounter the unknown. The difference is our mindset. If we're honest with ourselves, we will admit that the anxiety of the unknown isn't really about where we're going on this journey. It's about the lack of control we have in getting there. That's what gets us the most. We don't know anything about this unknown territory, and so we can't plan for it the way we want. We can't map out the route. Finishing will require us to leave the entire enterprise (more specifically, the results) to someone else. We have to trust the trip execution to God, and that means we have to trust His way.

Eh.

Honestly, I'm not thrilled with the notion of that. But let's reframe the way we see the unknown. The unknown can be known. In fact, the only way undone becomes done is if we get to know our unknown and trust the God of both.

Stop. Pause. Read that again. Slowly.

Stop actively avoiding the unknown. It's on the other side of the unknown that all your undone becomes done. It's where you finish.

P.S. Close your eyes right now and visualize where you could be a year from now if you embraced the unknown. Are you excited or anxious? Did you think about an amazing future or did you get stuck in a worst-case scenario? Write out what is specifically giving you anxiety.

20
The Waiting Game

"Change will not come if we wait for some other person or some other time. We are the ones we've been waiting for. We are the change that we seek."
President Barack Obama

Dear Finisher,

I am a professional *wait*-er. I can wait better than anyone I know. I'm your friend who loves waiting for a "sign." I wait to start. I wait to continue. I wait to finish. In my world, it's never the perfect time because we're "waiting" on it. I also corral other people into my shenanigans so I can say I'm waiting on them.

"Hey, Candace, when are you going to _____?"

"I'm just waiting on God."

That's a favorite.

It's also a convenient way to make my waiting sound "paraclete-ish" rather than what it is—punkish. Plus, it gets the religious folk off of me because who can argue with "waiting on God?"

I'm such a crafty Christian, aren't I?

Here's a tip: **stop the over-spiritualization of waiting**.

If I'm waiting, then I'm not doing that big scary thing that's freaking me out. If I'm waiting on someone else, then that can be my excuse as to why I'm not farther along my journey.

Sometimes collaboration is simply another person to blame if things belly up. Because if it's only me, there's only me to blame if things don't go well.

I know a girl. Let's call her Amina. Amina is a singer. She believes she's pretty good and has started a singing group. The members of the group keep dipping out and aren't very reliable or committed. Amina's friends and family tell her she should go solo, but she won't. She keeps trying to keep the group together, even though they are essentially dragging her down. Amina has big dreams of singing on stages all over the world. She dreams of fame. She writes the songs, but all the songs require three-part harmony. She will not leave the group behind and try for herself. You know what Amina's problem is? She is obviously hiding behind the group. But why? Well maybe if she has 'partners,' she can rely on them to take her where she wants to go. She can do less work. And if the group is shiftless and non-committal, she can lay all the culpability at their door, having a valid excuse not to progress while looking like the victim. Or she's scared that she's not as good a singer as she thinks she is, and in a group, she can conceal her individual and unique sound. Fear masquerading as humility.

Does any (or all) of that sound familiar?

Finisher, what are you waiting to do right now? *Who* are you waiting on? *What* are you waiting for? Really…what's the hold up? Why is it so hard to admit to ourselves that we're not about action? The truth is the admission is the only way we get free. We have to admit that we've been waiting and waiting and waiting…because we're scared of taking action (for whatever reason). Action requires consistency. It requires us to put ourselves out there. It requires us to deal with our excuses, ineptitudes, and platitudes.

I was supposed to have *been* started and finished a book! What was I waiting on? The perfect time? (Doesn't exist). To find a publisher first? (Why find a publisher for a book that isn't even started yet?) The perfect subject? (Not sure that exists either).

Yes, sometimes waiting isn't a bad thing. Not all waiting is bad. It's what you do with the waiting that determines whether it is serving you or your purpose. For a while, I was waiting without expectation. You know what that looks like? It looks like mundane, excuse-making, "I'm still praying on it" waiting. Purpose-less waiting. The last few years? It's been purpose-driven waiting for me. Before I started penning this book, I started two others. I wrote more on my blog. I started doing writing prompts to get my creative juices flowing. I got back in the habit of reading and started an online journal. I reached out to other creatives I admired to get advice. I started outlining chapters and went to a few #AllNightWrite events hosted by my now publisher, which helped me focus on my writing for 12 hours straight. Talk about gathering all my helps! This was all before I put one finger on this keyboard for *this* book. Sure, I prayed. But do you know what I prayed on? I didn't pray for the right time or for God to send me a sign. Truth be told, I had all the signs I needed. I didn't need another sign, sermon, or prophetic word. God was done talking. He'd said all He needed to say. So, I prayed that I would stop making excuses. I prayed that I would have the courage to face my waiting ways and overcome. I prayed against the spirit of fear. I prayed that I would believe in myself the way that my Father in heaven does. THAT is what waiting with expectation looks like.

There are for sure projects on my radar that will require collaboration. But this one? This is all me. God needs me to know

I can finish something on my own. He already knows I can, but He needs *me* to know I can.

Let's be honest and call a thing a thing. Most of us aren't waiting, we're stalling. We're hoping that if we keep delaying, the urge might go away or even that somehow, someway the "unfinished" will get finished without us. Some of us are hoping that if we just keep pushing it off, we won't want to do it anymore.

And some of us are far too comfortable on the sidelines. It's easier to yell at the player on the field from the comfort of our lounge chair. It's easier to criticize the work of someone else while stoutly refusing to put out our own work. Let me tell you how official my stall game is. I was using this book (this God-driven and purposeful project) to stall on moving forward in another area God has called me to. 'Cause I can only work on one purpose-driven project at a time, right?

Wrong!

So, I finally sent the email that I was "waiting" to send and was able to lock in a meeting. I told you, these letters are for me, too! God is getting us *both* together!

I am sick of waiting/stalling. Without realizing it, I wasn't just waiting to start the book or send the email. I was waiting for my life to really begin. My life is by no means terrible. There are aspects of my life that I absolutely love. But when it comes to living my life's purpose, I wasn't breathing it in and out on a daily basis. I was taking a gulp of air here and there. That's not enough.

Finisher, the only person who has you on hold is you. Turn that index finger around. Stop stalling and start moving in the direction of your dreams. Take real steps. Put yourself in the company of people who are doing what you're doing. Pray for mentors. If you have a problem being consistent in your project, it's probably not just relegated to that project. Start becoming consistent in other areas of your life. If you want to lose weight, start! Stop waiting for Monday or January or for a gym partner! Replace one soda or cup of juice with water! Stop stalling and do something! You'll NEVER finish if you keep waiting!

P.S. What is one thing you're stalling on right now? Take one scary action this week that will move you forward. Don't wait another moment!

To Wynter

"Wynter lived a fuller life than most people live in double her 38 years. Well done, babe. Well done. I celebrate you babe for an extraordinary life of giving to your children, me, and a world in need of hope. I love you and I always will. Your children will spend every day rising up and calling you blessed.
You have left an incredible legacy. I love you Beasy."
Jonathan Pitts

Dear Finisher,

These last few weeks have been awful and unproductive. An old-college friend of mine lost his wife suddenly. They were married for 15 years and have 4 daughters. While I know that nothing is perfect, they were a godly, beautiful family who I looked up to from afar. It spun me into a dark space. I cried most of the day I heard about it. To be honest, it shocked me. I only knew Wynter in passing. I reached out to her a few years ago when I saw her book come through my job. I sent her a message through social media with a picture saying how happy I was for her. We messaged back and forth a few times, and that was that. But hearing this news, it hit me hard. Through tear-stained eyes, I asked my husband, "What's the point?" I meant, what's the point of being happy or finishing *anything* if at any moment it can be snatched away from you? Why do we push to finish *any* race when our lives are not in our hands, and tragedy can strike at any moment? I am not an optimist. I am constantly waiting for the other shoe to drop. When good things happen in life, I lie in wait, ready for the inevitable bad. So what I've had to confront about myself lately is that I believe that bad things are meant to happen to me while good is just coincidence. And sadly, the news of my friend's passing solidified that thinking.

This belief system makes me scared to want more than what I currently have. The more I have, the more I have to lose. The more I love, the more heartbreak I can experience. The more pleasurable the experience, the more real the pain will be when it ends. If I don't push boundaries, then yes, I won't know great heights, but I also won't know what it is to fall to great depths. It's a terrible way to live, yet it's the only way I've known how to live. So, I've recently made a decision. I no longer want to sacrifice the certainty of my heights for unconfirmed reports of falling. And here's another truth: I'm going to have to will myself to believe that.

God didn't call us to live a safe life. Jesus lived a short life on this earth, but because "yes" was always on His lips, He made an eternal impact. His deeds, His words, and the impact He made in the lives closest to Him while He walked this earth? All finished. We can't control the time we have on this earth, but we can make sure we finish our purpose with the time we are allotted. I'm sure there are some who might have said that Jesus died early or too young. If He was on the earth longer, what more could He have done? But Jesus did what He came to do. Have you? How many yesses have you given to God this week? How much have you finished?

When I asked my husband "What's the point?" I didn't consider that the point is to do what God had planned for us to do. The point is to impact the people around us with our lives. The point is to do our deeds, speak God's truth, write the words, sing the songs, and impact the culture. We are designed to ascend our mountains. So let's give no thought to the valleys. Even if we end up there for a season, we should know that our Abba God will be there with us, too.

Yes, I was so saddened to hear about my friend's passing. She left a husband, four young kids, extended family, and an entire community to mourn her. But I also look at the legacy she left. She started a blog that turned into a full-blown ministry. She's been featured in magazines (and started her own). She wrote several books. And by all accounts, she was an amazing friend, wife, and mom. She represented Christ in it all. She didn't waste the time she was given. She was living to live again. Thank you, Wynter, for that lesson. May the legacy you left point us all to our own finish lines.

[Her] lord said unto [her], Well done, thou good and faithful servant: thou hast been faithful over a few things, I will make thee ruler over many things: enter thou into the joy of thy lord.
Matthew 25:21 KJV, *pronoun change mine*

P.S. How can we live in such a way that no matter how long we have on this earth, we can finish? What decisions can you make today that no matter how long you have, you can leave a legacy? Write down at least two.

22
A Tale of Two Baes

"Everything's changing around me / And I want to change too / It's one thing I know / It ain't cool being no fool."
The Roots, "Now or Never"

Dear Finisher,

Let me tell you a story about two people in my life. They are #FamiliarBae and #BeneficialBae. Familiar Bae and I were together for a really long time. They knew me inside and out. Being with them was so comfortable for me. But I started getting restless with Familiar Bae. I was trying to move forward, and Familiar Bae was chillin' with no intentions of trying to go to the next level. So, even though it was hard, I broke up with them. Not too long after, I started seeing Beneficial Bae. Beneficial Bae is EVERYTHING! They encourage me in my endeavors, push me when I need to be pushed, likes to take me out on the town, and is always so affectionate and affirming. BB loves to stunt for the 'gram! We posted last week about how happy we were together, and wouldn't you know a few days later, Familiar Bae slid into my DMs talking about "Hey Big Head. WYD?"

But seriously, there will be moments on this journey when past associations, past safety-nets, old go-to behaviors, and even some old romantic flings will find their way to you. Familiarity was working hard to get back my attention. Make no mistake, the closer you get to finishing, your past will make all the plays to pull you backwards. Tell your past that you are out here living your best life! Don't allow who you used to be and what you used to do to entice you to hustle backwards!

This is especially hard when you and your current dream are having some struggles. When the inspiration has worn off and perspiration hasn't shown up yet.

When you're struggling to make time.

When you're sitting on the couch with *Red Table Talk*, watching other people get their healing while you avoid your own.

Old patterns and behaviors will start looking good.

"Oh, Candace, this book doesn't matter. It's already been said and done."

"Oh, Candace. You're not different. Just settle into a 'regular' life like other people."

"Oh, Candace. You don't need to write today. Take a break. Take ALL the breaks."

"This offering doesn't matter. It won't help anyone. You're just blowing smoke."

"Don't you miss having direct deposit? Every two weeks."

"Remember how easy life used to be?"

Oooh. Familiar Bae is so raggedy.

The past often lies, painting an incomplete picture of what it actually looked like. My past tried to remind me of all the good times, the steady paychecks, the ease, the comfort. I almost went back. I told y'all I tried to get another job. I almost stopped writing this book because I was letting my past convince me that I would never be able to help anybody. And then, Holy Spirit reminded me of the truth, the complete picture. Oh yeah! My past used to use and abuse me and left me with bad credit!

#BoyBye

Don't let your past paint revisionist history for you. Familiar Bae has no intentions on seeing you finish. They aren't sending you good vibes or love and light. All they want to do is draw you back into old foolishness. They want you to stay in that stuck place with them. Don't fall for it. If you are a believer, think about the children of Israel (see book of Exodus). They were six weeks into their relationship with Beneficial Bae after groaning to God for 400 years about their terrible relationship with Familiar Bae. The journey toward freedom started getting rocky, and all of sudden, they were ready to go back! Don't start longing for the enslavement of Egypt because what you're currently encountering isn't what you thought it'd be. Don't let #FamiliarBae keep you from #BeneficialBae.

P.S. Who or what is the #FamiliarBae and #BeneficialBae of your life? Make a list of the pros and cons of staying with each. What did you uncover?

23
What's Your Motivation?

"Sometimes the sin isn't in the action, but the motivation behind it."
Candace E. Wilkins

Dear Finisher,

I've known a lot of finishers who *didn't* finish. Finishing was in them, as I've said in previous letters, but they could never actually accomplish it. The common thread is usually the degree of motivation a finisher has. If you jump from project to project without completing anything you start, consider your motivation. Why do you do what you do? Be honest with yourself. Are your motivations altruistic or are they motivated by some perceived deficiency? Some of us start things because we want to be seen. Some of us begin because we want to be validated externally. Some of us are fighting against the demons of the past or the father who told us we weren't worthy enough (by his words, actions, inactions, presence or lack thereof). Some of us are still trying to prove to others that we are 'somebody.' When we pursue fame or notoriety (especially for believers), it is usually short-lived or eludes us altogether.

If your motivation is rooted in self-glory, you'll find yourself in an addictive cycle. In fact, once the feeling of "being known" fades, you'll chase your next high. God has a habit of hiding people before He uses them, and too many of us refuse to be hidden. We'll do anything to be seen. We'll hop from social media platform to platform, commenting on everybody's everything, trying to market ourselves. We'll try to duplicate other people's platforms that we envy. We'll beg for attention, borrow money, and steal ideas! We'll jump on whatever is trending, whatever the fad is, just so someone can call our name—not realizing that the Creator of the universe already knows our name. That's who we should seek to be known by.

Fame is an illusion. It won't fill that emptiness in you. Let us stop chasing the uncatchable. I remember someone spoke God's word over me and said, "Your gift will make room for you and bring you before great men." In my alone time, God followed up with, "The issue isn't that you get in the room; it's what you do when you get in there." Promotion doesn't come from the east or the west; it comes from God. We've got to stop pushing our way to the front, led only by our fragile egos, and cosigning God's name to our chicanery. In the body of Christ, how often are we receiving words of reproof? When's the last time a prophet came to town and told you that it was your "season to be unknown?" Yeah, we don't hear that too much. When's the last time God said He was hiding you indefinitely. When was the last time He said the idea you have wasn't for "the nations"? What if it's for the neighborhood? What if you're Jonathan to someone's David? (See their story in 1 & 2 Samuel). Could you push someone else's God-given purpose above your own positioning? What if you're Mary's Elizabeth? (See Luke 1:39) Could you prophesy and speak life to what someone else is carrying with an understanding that what they've got might have more far-reaching impact? I reckon that a lot of us wouldn't be. Some of us can't finish because we're too busy trying to be the head when God called us to be the arm. Or the lungs. Or the blood. We're grasping at being known and working outside of our gifting while doing so.

I remember when I was growing up in my home church. The person who made the biggest impact on me wasn't my pastor. He was the most well-known for sure, but for me, the people who laid the biggest foundation for me were two women: Betty Jean Scott and Virginia Brooks. One was my daycare provider and second mother, and the other was my Sunday school teacher. They weren't the head, but they were certainly the blood, lungs, and internal organs of my church. Without them, I would not be who I am today.

Sometimes, the hard work that we do isn't seen by the masses or recognized by those in power. Would you still work hard? Would you still put the work out? Maybe your area of gifting is such that no one ever knows your name on IG, but the impact you're making is written in the annals of heaven and embedded in the lives of those you've touched.

Where does our obsession with fame and notoriety stem from? What I've found is that too many of us find it difficult stand firm in whoever we are and what we do, especially if it's something that's away from the limelight and doesn't earn us applause. It's probably one of my biggest struggles: to not depend on the claps. We have a codependent relationship with recognition, and social media only makes it worse. If no one can see my posts about what I'm doing daily, did I do it? Did it get still done? I purposely stayed off social media regarding writing this book and only told a few key people. Why? Because I'm not immune to wanting people to "see" me. I'm a creative whose love language is words. You think bowing at the altar of external affirmation eludes me? It doesn't. I want people to clap for me, too. But Finisher, I can't live for their claps because then I'll die by their silence. My motivation for finishing must come from some place internal and worshipful, not of me but of the God I serve. There has to be something in me that wants to finish this in order to serve something larger than my ego. The act of finishing should be enough for me without a barrage of folks singing my praises. Furthermore, the finished product ought to be, most importantly, glorifying to an audience of one: God.

P.S. Be honest with yourself: Why do you want to finish what you're currently working on? Make a list of TRUE reasons you want to finish. Take stock of how many have to do with external validation.

24
Tell the Truth (Especially to Yourself)

"Have the boldness to tell yourself the truth; every bit of it."
Oprah Winfrey

Dear Finisher,

This letter is brought to you by a conversation that went down in one of my group chats. We were discussing a post we saw on FB from a person who was passive-aggressively coming at another individual for how they've treated them. The post wasn't really the problem. The content was. It was odd that the very thing the person was accusing the other person of doing to them was what they do to others. I said, "The level of people's self-deception is astounding." And that's true. The stories people will create to insulate themselves firmly in victimhood blows my mind! This must be a consideration, Finisher. If you're always the victim or hero in every story you tell, you have a problem. You can be a finisher or a victim. Pick one because you cannot be both.

Sometimes, we're the villain in the story, and we need to face that. Sometimes, we are the a-hole. We are the ones who told the lie to save face. We are the ones who said the hurtful thing to project a toughness we didn't feel. We are the people who avoided a person because we didn't want to "hear it." We were the ones who wrecked the relationship. We were the ones who were unkind or had a nasty attitude. We were apathetic when we could have been passionate. We were the ones who held ourselves back. We were the antagonist in the story: someone else's and, often times, our own.

I once knew a girl named Lara. She made some bad choices in her life. She made some good choices, too. She only wanted credit for the good though. The bad choices she blamed on upbringing, her parents, her current circumstances, and God. She tended to date the wrong types of men, never seeing that *she* may have been a contributing factor in those decisions. She has friends in her life who care about her and who she cares about, but she can at times be a bit mean and standoffish. Whenever anyone tries to give her advice or call her to the carpet, she blame-shifts or plays the victim. She's done some good things in her life, but she's not quite found her purpose. Whenever anyone inquires about it, she puffs out her chest and lists any number of impressive accomplishments. She's got a lot in her life to be thankful for, but she only sees what's not there. She lies to cover up what she's scared everyone can see. She can be prideful. And ungrateful. Jealous. Mean-spirited. Selfish.

I have at times been Lara. She is me. Could she be you, too?

I started my first few letters to you with how I needed to face some hard truths about myself. It wasn't easy. It *isn't* easy. You can't finish if you're still in denial about the reasons you don't finish. It takes vulnerability and self-awareness. You cannot and will not finish if you spend most of the time denying and covering up why you struggle to finish. Take off the mask. Stop aestheticizing every time an ugly part of you is revealed. Put down your drug of choice. Put those tears away if they only serve to manipulate an emotional reaction from someone trying to hold you accountable. God isn't put-off by your secret failures and inclinations, but what He cannot do (and He will not do) is push an imposter to the finish line. Only the real you can finish.

And here's a hard truth: sometimes those closest to us can really see us. If you've got some true-blue close friends, and you are currently lying (or in denial) about some aspect of your life and personality, trust me, they know! You're not hiding it. They see it. We see it.

Some of us have insulated ourselves from critique by our hardened hearts. I saw an IG post the other day that asked people "What was your first impression of me?" and then it said, "Watch what you say to me! Don't say nothing to the left or I'm coming for you." So you ask for the truth and then put up all kinds of roadblocks to hearing anything that isn't favorable to you?

Like...*what?*

Finishing requires truth. One phrase that has been resonating in my spirit for the past few weeks is *face your trauma.* I've been spending time in prayer for other people and much of what I pray about is for them being able to face their trauma. There is truth in your trauma. It's a scary notion, for sure. To have to go back to what hurt, harmed, or even tried to kill you, dig it up, sit down with its decomposed and rotting body, interview it so you can understand the damage that it did to you, and then—wait for it—carry that mess back to the grave and bury it. Then you have to remind yourself that the trauma *is* dead and stop breathing life back into it. Behind every finisher (that struggles to finish and even the ones that don't) is a living breathing trauma that we won't face. For me, I had to stop acting like my stuff wasn't there. I sat with it and let the truth be revealed to me. I stopped avoiding it. I stopped shielding it with my pride.

I understand that it's beyond difficult to realize that maybe we're the problem. Maybe it's not everyone else. Maybe it's not your spouse's fault. Maybe you're the one with problematic behavior. Maybe it's your issues that aren't allowing you to be successful or move forward. Maybe the reason you can't sustain a healthy relationship is connected to your dad not being around. Maybe your mom died at a critical age, and you struggle to know who you are. Maybe that's why it's hard for you to trust others, or even yourself. Acknowledging these truths doesn't mean you sit in the security of blame. You can accept where it started and how it's impacted you and still take responsibility for your own actions and how it plays out in your life currently. Maybe your trauma isn't fatherlessness or molestation (like mine), but there is likely something that stops you from being the best version of yourself. Be willing to figure it out.

Sometimes, as finishers who struggle to finish, we can think it must be sweeter on the other side. We want to be the go-getter so badly. It must be great to push through goals without impediment (or so we think). Not necessarily. Trauma can be found in many ways. If that go-getter is *killing* themselves to meet every deadline, driving themselves into the ground mentally and physically to excel in everything they touch, is that healthy? Because sometimes behind all that hard work is a person who feels they aren't good enough, that they'll never measure up. Maybe a person who feels like they don't deserve to rest, that even in moments of celebration they're already looking to the next thing they need to conquer. They might be a person who mostly attaches their value to what they accomplish. Now, don't be annoying trying to diagnose all your go-for-the goal friends (they're not all like this), but in some cases, while productivity can look pretty, it can sometimes be trauma wearing a mask that's more palatable to the outside world. We can be productive but depressed. We can be productive but not whole. Hell, we can be productive and not finish. (Remember busy-ness vs. business?)

I've watched people not be able to celebrate themselves; not be able be alone; not be able to sustain a healthy stable relationship with others (romantic and platonic); not be able to tell the truth; not be able to stand on their own without someone affirming their decisions; or, not be able to hear criticism. Those same people can be hyper-critical of others, abusive to themselves and others, take drugs to numb pain, or meander aimlessly through life. The list goes on and on.

For me, I'm controlling because I'm scared of what happens if I just trust God and let Him lead. (I've already lost a father! What else can happen?). I have allowed fear to take up residence in my life because new experiences require me to put myself out there, and what if I'm rejected? I already told you about my escape and safety issues. If you talk to my friends and husband, I'm sure they could come up with a million more. The bottom line? I've had to be willing to face all of this. I was so sick and tired of the merry-go-round of foolishness in my own life that I decided to finally deal with trauma. I took a shovel, a flashlight, and walked to the graveyard. I was determined to dig this stuff up and deal with it all so I could be free.

Be willing to face the truth, Finisher. Some of us avoid therapy because we know it'll make us responsible for our own actions. It's far easier to keep blaming the man, Mama, or the multitudes. Be courageous enough to hear the truth about yourself — whether it comes straight from God, a good friend, a therapist, or some IG followers. You cannot finish without hearing the truth. The whole truth. The good, the bad, and the fearfully held back. May we be compassionate truth-tellers, but more importantly, may we be dispassionate truth-receivers.

P.S. Go to a really good friend or another trusted source who loves you. Ask them why they think you struggle to finish. Be open to receiving the truth.

25
Comparison Kills

"Comparison is an act of violence against the self."
Iyanla Vanzant

Dear Finisher,

Lately, Jonathan McReynolds' album *Make More Room* has been on constant rotation. That thing *bangs*! I've been sitting in a coffee shop, listening to every song, and having a full-on worship moment. There's a particular song on it called "Comparison Kills."

Chile.

Brother Jonathan got me all the way together, you hear me?

All the lyrics in that song are so amazing, but there is one verse that keeps tapping my soul.

The grass is fine/'Til it looked greener on the other side/Now you're believing that you fell behind/But why try to match what should be one of a kind?/You're one of a kind/We all wanna be successful/And get mad when God's not in a rush/Waste your time just making copies/You'll see you did not accomplish much.

Comparison, I've found, has done the most damage and been the worst pariah in my ability to progress. There is nothing worse than trying to run your race and get to *your* finish line while simultaneously worrying about the next person's race.

Wondering where they got their running outfit from.

Questioning why your race has hurdles and theirs doesn't.

Trying to figure out if they started before or after you.

All we're essentially doing is looking to the left or the right and, in the meantime, slowing up our own progress. Listen, I struggle with comparing my journey to others, too. I'm telling you what I know. I know what it is to look at someone else's marriage, house, career, Instagram feed, children, etc. and wonder why it's not mine. But really, is it that I want *their* lives, or am I just simply showing a dissatisfaction with my own? With the choices I've made? With the hand I've been dealt? Each person's journey is their own, and most of the time, we're only seeing the highlight reel. Unless people make a point to show us, we are only ever seeing the good parts, never the underbelly. And even if people talk about the hardships they went through, we only focus on the victory that we see from them today because that's the part we want. Often, we want victory-*lite*. We covet what the hardship, discipline, prayer, tears, and arguments afforded them but can't actually handle the hardship, discipline, prayer, tears or arguments. And if we really *knew* people's stories, most of us wouldn't have been able to handle the weight of their struggle!

Do you understand that God created you not only with your purpose in mind but also with your inevitable struggles in mind, too? God knew what you'd go through, how long you'd go through it, what'd you need to go through it, and you were equipped specifically to be able to handle it!

"Should be..." is the enemy of all progress. I cannot even tell you how many times I capitulated to the standard of where I "should be." I should have *been* an author. I should have *been* gotten married. I should have *been* had kids. I should have *been* finished. How is that helpful? And who says? Who is creating this timeline of where you *ought* to be? Whoever THEY are should be taken behind the woodshed. I am so exhausted of worshipping at that altar. Where I'm at is where I am. My journey is my own, and I refuse to spend one more ounce of energy living my life for anyone else other than the God I say I serve. When we stew in comparison, we're worshipping someone else's life, timeline, and journey. We are resting in a lie that our life could be another way. Yeah, sure. Maybe it could have been another way, but it isn't, for whatever reason.

Some of us are making decisions right now (mostly bad) so we can try to make up for what we perceive as lost time. We are running our races and trying to move forward with a rear-facing and side-eyeing viewpoint. Is it any wonder we're not further along on our own journey? I've gotten to a point where I'm resolved to run my race and rest in God's plans for me. I don't want to keep up with the Kardashians, my friends, my family, my foes, IG influencers, Huey, Dewey, Louie, or any other members of Donald Duck's family. I'm built for my journey, and I will not leave this earth having lived to make other people envious of my life or trying to acquire other folks' blessings, thinking it will make me happy. I will not perform happiness. I will simply *be* happy.

You cannot finish your own race trying to "win" someone else's! And what's the prize if you win?! Probably one you don't even want because it wasn't your race to win to begin with. Run *your* race and guess what? You can't be behind. You winning your race is inevitable. You know why? Because you're the only one running it.

P.S. Listen to Jonathan McReynolds' song "Comparison Kills" and journal what comes to you when listening.

26
We don't have TIME to finish

"Those who make the worst use of their time are the first to complain of its brevity."
Jean de La Bruyère, Les Caractères

Dear Finisher,

We've all told this lie: "I don't have time!"

I've said this many times myself, and let's be honest, *sometimes* it's true. *Sometimes*, a person asks something of me, and I legitimately do not have time to do it. *Sometimes*, I am having a busy day or week, and I cannot work that particular "thing" into my schedule. Life happens. *However*, I resolutely believe we use "lack of time" as an excuse not to finish. We all have 24 hours in a day. And trust me, I am clear that we have stuff on our schedules that cannot be avoided or changed. In some ways, our time isn't even our own. It may belong to our jobs, our spouses, our parents, our kids, etc. But I am also just as clear that we don't always manage the time we do have in the most productive manner. An old boss of mine made me do an inventory of how I spent my time during the work day. I broke it down minute by minute, what I was doing. While I hated doing it at the time, it was helpful for me to see what I spent the most time on. It also helped me to see how distracted I get during the day. There were times when I'd interrupt a task with another task and, at the end of the day, neither task got done. If I were to do that exercise today, I'd likely see my writing broken up by Instagram (a scroll here and a scroll there). Or I'd see a movie playing in the "background" while I write only to realize that my writing was actually the background activity. With the time I have left after the imperative, how much of that time is spent on the worthwhile pursuit of finishing? If I'm truthful with myself, not even 30%. Yes, I'm writing this book on finishing, but I'm probably the undisputed, worldwide champion of Time Wasters Incorporated! I waste time better than anyone I know. And it's not that I don't have time, it's that I spend the time I *do* have doing everything but finishing.

Here's the thing: we have the time to finish. I'd go as far as to say, if finishing was our priority, we'd find the time to do it. We'd make the time. So maybe we need to just say it out loud so we can deal with it: "Finishing is not my priority right now." Let's deal with that reality instead of acting like it's not true. When anyone says they don't have time, what I often hear is "That's not my priority right now." Why? Well, if, God forbid, we got gravely ill and had to go to the hospital for a treatment three times a week (without which we'd die), I'd bet most of us would find time. Because setting aside that time would be necessary for us to stay alive. Well, Finisher, is your purpose — finishing that thing you know God gave you to do — not just as important for your living?

I got my feelings hurt one day while washing dishes. I heard in my spirit, "If you have time to be social, you have time to be studious." I mean, it's true. I watch people say, "I don't have time to do this or that," and then the very next day, watch their

IG and FB Lives where they are partying or hopping a plane for a trip here or there.

Sidebar: I'm not mad at anyone for the self-care of vacations, fun, or rest. They are critical. They are vitally important. Self-care bubble baths, self-care pedicures, self-care motorcycle riding, self-care do-nothing, self-care glasses of wine, self-care essential oils, self-care dance parties, self-care exercise, self-care eat-right, self-care eat-cake — I am here for it all. But when are we going to make time for the self-care of finishing? When does self-care finishing happen? When are we going to make the revolutionary act of finishing what we start a priority so we have a better quality of life?

Because let me tell you what self-care is NOT. It is *not* having a project hanging over your head so that you can hardly enjoy your day trip to the wine country. Self-care is *not* backing off from relationships that get difficult or challenge you so that you never have anyone to enjoy the wine country with. Self-care is *not* wasting away precious hours finding your light, taking pictures of your hands placed just right on your laptop with the hashtag #workinghard because it's easier to *look* productive than *be* productive. Self-care is *not* being there for everyone else but yourself.

Sometimes, we make time for everybody else but ourselves. We're out here trying to be super-wife, super-partner, super-sister, super-brother, super-friend, super-birthing other people's dreams. WHEN ARE YOU GOING TO MAKE TIME TO SHOW UP FOR YOURSELF?! When are you going to take time to birth your own dreams? When are you going to make yourself a priority? Listen, this may ruffle some feathers, but let me tell you what my past weekend looked like. On Saturday, I was invited to a one-day church conference whose registration fee was only

$10. (I know! That's unheard of!). I also had plans to go to my church on Sunday. I created a to-do list on Friday night and figured out that the coming week would need to be a heavy writing week because I had deadlines I needed to meet. Yes, I had places I *wanted* to go but based on what I needed to get done on that to-do list, I decided against the conference. On Saturday, I spent some time with my hubby (because as I said, heavy writing week), made up a curry chicken for the week (because leftovers are life), and washed all the dishes. That evening, I looked at that to-do list and knew I could either attend church OR spend that time getting work done.

I decided to get my stuff done.

I know, I know. Every pastor reading this is cringing.

I spent the entire day in the house, cleaning, organizing, and getting myself prepared for the week. When I laid myself down at about 10 p.m. (with a to-do list that was almost completely crossed off), I knew I had made the right decision. Just because I didn't attend that conference or go to church on Sunday doesn't mean I didn't spend time with Jesus. I did so right in my home. And frankly, sometimes the most sacred, Jesus-loving thing we can do is take time to get our house in order. He doesn't stop speaking once we drive off the church parking lot. God had a lot to say to me while I was washing dishes.

We must steward our time better. This may mean we can't attend everybody's everything. Sometimes we're always out because we're scared if we're not there, we're going to miss something. If we don't get our FOMO (fear of missing out) selves together! Say no, Finisher. For me, one thing I will no longer do is show up for other people at the expense of showing up for myself. That doesn't mean I just flat-out stop showing up to events, but it does mean I schedule my time in such a way that being there for others (in whatever capacity) is not hindering my own production. Time is like money... if you don't tell it where to go, you'll wonder where it went. It might mean saying no to another project to focus on the one I should be doing. Sometimes, it means staying in the house and getting my life in order instead of trying to rush and get everything done in four hours on a Sunday night. At times, it has meant foregoing that beloved after-church nap to stay up. And I can assure you that it definitely means not spending two hours scrolling on FB, IG, or YouTube.

Put your phone down, Finisher!

Some of us would change the world if we took certain apps off our phones.

To be clear: the issue isn't usually *if* you have the time to finish; it's likely whether you're going to *make* the time to finish. It's probably an issue of whether you're going to use the time you *do* have to finish. Be honest about what distracts you, and make serious changes to that end.

When I'm writing (or trying to finish anything really), the only thing I can have on is a playlist. Sometimes, I need complete silence. I can't have a "background" movie on. It's sometimes best to even close other tabs on my computer—especially the ones that blink to tell me there's a new message. My phone has to be away from me, charging. When I take a break, I need it timed so I don't look up two hours later and wonder what happened. And sometimes, if I'm in a groove, I may not be able to take a break. Maybe I can't get up until I've met my goals for the day. Or, maybe I do take a break, but I'll stay up a little later to meet my goal. The other night, I wanted to hit a deadline so badly, I stayed up until 7 a.m. to do it. Now, I'm not suggesting you do that, but I AM saying, *Temporary inconvenience for permanent improvement.* Whatever the sacrifice, we have the time. Let's stop saying you don't. In fact, let's be totally real. At this point, you don't have time *NOT* to finish.

P.S. Create your own time inventory. Clock the minutes of your day in written form. Can you 'find' time to finish?

27
Who's in Your Crew?

"Tell me who you walk with, and I'll tell you who you are."
Esmeralda Santiago

Dear Finisher,

In a previous letter, I discussed accountability and how important it is to have people around you who can serve in that capacity. But beyond those who are specifically there to help push to you toward the finish line, who do you surround yourself with in general? Who's in your crew? It cannot be overstated how important it is to have good folks in your corner. We were never meant to do life alone. From Genesis to Revelation, God shows us how important community is. Listen, even Jesus had a crew and then a few within the crew who were closer still.

I've always had a crew because I've always wanted one. My mom has had the same circle of friends since high school. I've watched them endure arguments with each other, marriages and divorces, raising kids and grandkids, job promotions and retirements, sickness, health, and death. Through it all, and while they drive each other crazy, for the most part, they remain together. This is always something I've admired and desired. In my life, I have a group of friends I've had since college (Hey

Divas!), and God has also brought wonderful additions into my life in the form of brothers I acquired through marriage (Hey Dons!); sisters and mentors I've made along the journey; couple-friends that hubby and I have together; church family we adore; coworkers who became family; South Philadelphia neighbors who became cousins, aunts, and uncles; social media family (yes, they count!); and our blood families! I count myself extremely blessed because I'm surrounded by a lot of love. Every circle mentioned has played a role in our (me and hubby) lives in a variety of ways. You would not be getting these letters if it were not for these communities of people who have impacted me in concrete ways. I have needed every single check-in, group-chat hype session, inspirational IG post, and altar-shaking prayer to get me to this point. I've also needed every "life gathering" session, every rebuke, every silent reproof, and chastisement.

But, community isn't easy. Isolation can sometimes feel like a blessed relief—I get that. In isolation, the only person we have to deal with is ourselves. And to be honest, sometimes, we can have friends but keep them at a distance so we don't have to deal with other folks' mess (or more acutely, so that they can't see ours). I've seen this happen countless times in the church. We are so careful to maintain our manicured images to match our titles that sometimes we can't seek help in the very place we're supposed to be able to go for it. We keep folks at a distance, not letting people see how jacked up we really are. How silly of us to be in the hospital, walking around with Stage 4 Cancer, in the place of treatment, hiding our sickness while playing doctor to everyone else. There is only one Great Physician, folks. And that Great Physician can heal it all, even those emotional wounds we're trying so hard to hide under those titles.

There have been times in my own life when I pushed away those closest to me so that they couldn't see my foolishness. I thought that if they saw how deeply flawed I was, the ways I feel less-than, my triggers or my *isms*, they wouldn't be my friend anymore, or they'd use the information against me at my most vulnerable.

Can I be real? Sometimes, that happened. And it hurt.

Sometimes, we keep people around us who don't challenge us to be better. If every person in your life is just like you, thinks just like you, acts just like you, and agrees with everything you say, where's the bar to grow to be better? And, how boring!

In my circles, I count myself to be one of the least successful. I don't say that as a point of contention, I say it as inspiration to be better. And not better than them. Better than the me I was yesterday. To keep going after my dreams. To get closer to God. To make decisions from a place of power, not pain. It doesn't mean that my community is perfect. Far from it. It's filled with imperfect people who live imperfect lives. Sometimes, we hurt each other, sometimes intentionally. Sometimes, we're not there for each other in the ways we should be. We stumble. We fall (out) and maybe fall back in. One lesson I'm currently learning (and it's a hard one) is to be open to the way my communities shift and change. I used to be opposed to letting people enter or exit my life. After prayerful reconsideration, I now am allowing my community to change shape as I do. I'm not on the no-new friends train or even the keep-the-old-friends-at-all-costs train. I'm on the discern-what-my-life-needs train because that's the one that's on track to finish.

P.S. Think about who's in your crew. Write out their names and their positive qualities vs. the foolery they bring to your life. Adjust accordingly.

28
The Audacity of Hope

"My hope is built on nothing less than Jesus' blood and righteousness. I dare not trust the sweetest frame but wholly lean on Jesus' name."
Edward Mote

"Skepticism is just hope that's been beat down."
Candace E. Wilkins

Dear Finisher,

I have never read President Barack Obama's book, *The Audacity of Hope*. That said, when I think about hope, it's this phrase that pops into my head.

Audacity is the willingness to take bold risks. We tend to think of hope as this beautiful experience, but sometimes, it's not. Hope can be scary. I regularly grapple with the notions of hope. Once I finish these letters, and they go to my publisher, all I have left to do is hope. It's a jarring proposition. I have to hope that what I've done is received well by my editor. I have to hope that I don't have to completely start over. And then the scariest hope of all: I hope that what I'm putting out into the world is received well and that it helps someone to their own finish line.

What if none of that happens?

I'm sitting here finishing these letters, with my community hyping me up from the sidelines. God is in my ear speaking good news, Husbae is out here swelling my head, and all I can think is, *What am I doing?* Crazy, right? My fear of hope has me actually trying to talk myself down. Trying to make sure I don't believe in any future goodness yet unseen or acquired.

When you've lived a little bit and have been disappointed on more than one occasion, having hope is hard. When I was a doe-eyed teenager and even in my 20s, it was easier to hope. Life hadn't kicked me down yet. My hope hadn't been deferred yet. When you've hoped for an event/a person/a pursuit/a property to come to fruition in your life, and it doesn't, it leaves an indelible impression on you. It makes you cautious about believing again.

I remember when I got my acceptance letter to Drexel University. Oh my goodness, I was so excited and filled with hope! I could legit hear my heartbeat in my eardrums. Up until that point in my life, there wasn't really anything that I'd gone for in life that I hadn't gotten. I remember going to sleep that night with my future completely planned out in my head. It never occurred to me that the next few years wouldn't look like what I planned/dreamed at all.

I wouldn't finish that corporate communications degree.

I wouldn't get a high-paying job in my field. (Don't ask me what I wanted *to do* with that degree because, in truth, I had no idea.)

I wouldn't meet my husband in college and marry him right after graduation.

I wouldn't have babies in my mid to late twenties.

That mansion I was promised numerous times in the M-A-S-H game, hasn't happened. Yet.

My hopes were dashed. And so, I stopped hoping. I squelched one of the best parts of who I was because I was over being disappointed. I settled for good enough and sometimes not even that. I settled for low-hanging fruit, stuff that didn't require much hope. As a dreamer and a visionary, dashed hopes have imprisoned my heart and stifled my creativity more than procrastination, lack of discipline, and fear combined. It taught me to keep my aspirations to a minimum, to dream small and keep life attainable.

To be honest, there's hardly anything that hurts more than unfulfilled hope. The Bible actually says, "Hope deferred makes the heart sick but when desire comes, it is the tree of life" (see Proverbs 13:12). My heart has been sick on many occasions. But here is what I learned: I was focused on the wrong thing. I was hoping in a particular outcome rather than in the God of the outcome. My hope wasn't in Jesus; it was in the expected end. Don't get me wrong, there's nothing wrong with believing in good outcomes. There's nothing wrong with believing that God's got great things planned for your life. Living life without hope is a terrible reality. Cynicism and skepticism become your portion. But I don't ever want to place anything acquired above not just His plans for my life but just Him. So, it's not about denying ourselves hope; it's about making sure hope remains in the right place. Whenever you hope, you risk disappointment. It's why hope is such an audacious enterprise. But if you ultimately hope and believe that the best plan (even if it's not the one you initially wanted) will succeed, hope isn't so scary after all.

Scratch that. It's still scary. But I promise you can trust the God of hope. God's record on that is GOOD.

P.S. Hope again.

29
To those who endure...

"We give up too soon.
The sure way to succeed is to endure to the very end."
Lailah Gifty Akita

Dear Finisher,

There have been days when I've wanted to quit writing these letters. Who knew I had even one letter worth of information to share much less forty? Most days, I ask myself why. Why would I keep doing this to myself? Why am I putting myself through this torture of writing? There were days when I just stared at the screen and nothing would come. Even after gathering the helps, after having an amazing writing day the previous day, after getting myself hopped up on tasty coffee, or having the exact right writing playlist—nothing would come. No matter how many times my husband would hold me accountable or how many FB friends would check on my writing, some days it was agonizing opening my laptop.

Last night, I was reading a book, and I started to see some of the things I've written to you about in this book. It really discouraged me. I was back at "What's the point?" I really started to hate this whole project. Sure, there have been great triumphs, but there have also been more times when I've awakened to feelings of defeat before I even attempted to start. In those moments, I want to give up.

This is what finishing really looks like. There will inevitably come a point when we are almost at our finish line, and we take our foot off the gas. We slow down. We're exhausted. We don't know where we're going to muster up the strength to go on. We are tired. We are weary in our well-doing. We legit don't want to do it anymore. We say things like, "Why did I even start this?"

I'm in several business FB groups. One day, I was scrolling through my feed, and I saw a post by a business owner who was celebrating a huge win for her business. A celebrity had posted her products (without being asked), and she said her orders were through the roof. What got me was this: she said that the year prior she was in the same group asking if she should keep going or shut it down. She said her business wasn't financially doing well, and she was tired. She thanked the group for encouraging her *to endure.*

Finishing these letters to you has been one of the most arduous tasks I've ever undertaken. This past year has been one long test in endurance. Could I stick it out? Well, apparently, I did since you are holding the book. But there were days when I didn't think I would.

I remember sitting in my public library, surrounded by books, and wondering, *how many of these authors felt like this?* I would venture to say at least 90% of them. And yet, here their books sit. Done. Completed. What separates them from some of us? They kept going despite being surrounded by reasons/excuses to quit.

Hebrews 12:1 says, "Therefore, since [I AM] surrounded by such a great cloud of WITNESSES, let [ME] throw off everything that hinders and the sin that so easily entangles, and let [ME] run with perseverance the race marked out for [ME] (changes and additions mine). Those books in that library were my cloud of witnesses. Finisher, feed your exhaustion with witnesses, not excuses. They persevered, and therefore, I knew I could, too. We endure not because it's just inherent in us to do so. We endure because we dare to stick with it—whatever *it* is—when hanging on by a thread, when we no longer feel love toward *it*, and when we're exhausted of fighting for *it*.

Endurance isn't the perfect race with the perfect time finished strong. Endurance is more times a hellish race, a worn-out body, perhaps a late start with an even later finish. It's watching others run past you. It's seeing all of that, knowing all of that, yet choosing to put one foot in front of the other until we see tape. Endurance is about outlasting the feeling to quit.

It's two and a half weeks before I must turn in my first draft to my editor, and I have writer's block. My writing has come to a dead stop. I wrote the first part of this letter months ago, and I now find myself going through previous chapters, making notes. I could have given it up. I wanted to give up. But then I decided to tell you what was happening, and my writing block has ended. Just like that. I resolved to endure, and I did.

P.S. That thing you put down because you didn't think you could make it through, pick it back up and continue on. What does picking it up look like today? Endure, Finisher.

30

Procrastination

"Procrastination is the art of keeping up with yesterday."
Don Marquis

Dear Finisher,

Do you procrastinate? I do. Badly. I've been doing it almost my whole life. When I was in high school and college, I used to get a rush out of it. There was something about waiting until the last minute and being up all night that seemed to make my creativity flow. But as I've gotten older, I don't get the same rush from procrastinating that I used to. It doesn't make my creativity flow; it makes me feel anxious and out of control. So why is it such a tough habit to break? First, procrastination can be very alluring.

I am a staller by nature. I will avoid until I can't avoid anymore. And usually, I only procrastinate with things that I'm anticipating will be difficult or require more of me than I am willing to give. So, I wait. And wait. And then, when I can't wait anymore, I start working. It usually means I'm up late, or waking up early, hovered over my desk typing as fast as I can or researching a topic with my back to the proverbial wall. Does any of that sound fun? It's not. But, inevitably, it gets done. I turn it in, or I get through the presentation, and all I remember is the high of crossing the finish line. I don't remember how terrible everything leading up to it was. The stress. The anxiety. Then I get hit upside the head with a hard truth that I recently read on the Internet. The quote is from Bishop Rosie O'Neal who said, "Procrastination is the arrogant assumption that God owes you another chance to do tomorrow what He gave you the chance to do today." So despite the allure of procrastination, the rush or high, the truth is, tomorrow is legit not promised to any of us. I know people say it all the time, but it really is true. But even deeper than that, tomorrow's time isn't promised.

Procrastination is the action of delaying or postponing something. We know that. But have you ever thought about how it relates to the biblical principle of sowing and reaping? When we procrastinate in our creative process, the projects that come from that or even our decision-making, we are actually sowing delay. Then we sit around and tell God to hurry up and get us to our destiny. Some of us have been postponing so many things, not realizing that we will reap the harvest of those postponements. I've seen this truth in my own life. When I stopped putting "it" off (whatever it happened to be), life started moving at a quicker pace. It's not that God had me on hold. I had myself on hold. We sow delay, we reap delay.

One of the major issues I now see with procrastination is that when I've waited to do something tomorrow that I could have done today, I miss the opportunity of what God could have filled tomorrow with. I can't be fully open to the possibilities of tomorrow because it's already filled with today's work. When we keep procrastinating, we deny ourselves possibilities and dump worry all over our creative processes. The "high" of procrastination is no longer conducive to the productive life I'm trying to live, nor can I afford to eat the fruit thereof. I want each day to be filled with God's fresh plans for the day — not warmed up leftovers from the day before.

P.S. Write down some of the reasons you find yourself procrastinating. Are any of the reasons healthy or sustainable for the future you're trying to have?

31
Relationship Issues

"The first draft reveals the art, revision reveals the artist."
Michael Lee

Dear Finisher,

As I've been on this journey toward finishing, many of my relationships (friendships/acquaintances/social media relationships/church/marriage) are in a state of flux. This is because I am doing an inventory of who/what is necessary in my space. If I'm honest, when I see someone explaining how they are taking stock of their relationships, I roll my eyes. I do this because these people are usually "taking stock" every year and are always referring to the "haters" in their lives. Cue up my eye roll. That's not what's going on here, I assure you. Most of what I'm doing is curating my space and making honest assessments of where everyone needs to "land" in my life. But in doing this, one question I keep asking of myself is this: Is any particular or specific issue worth sacrificing the entire relationship? Whether it's deciding to click that unfollow/block button, stay friends, leave the church, or leave my own house, it always comes back to that. Is this thing that's currently vexing me worth backing off the relationship completely?

Frankly, sometimes, it is.

Some social media relationships are ones that I'm not very invested in. So when I see something problematic, I will unfollow them quick! But in real life, it's not that easy, and it shouldn't be. Be clear: I'm not advocating staying in abusive relationships. Absolutely *not*! But I do think there is a distinct difference between abuse and upset. In any relationship worth having, there is bound to be some upset. If you tuck tail and run every time you encounter it, you're never going to see anything through—including your creative pursuits. Do you realize that you're in a relationship with your project? You most certainly are. And that project is going to have all the same symptoms of any other relationship. At the beginning, you're in the honeymoon phase. Every little discovery is amazing. All flaws are overlooked. Every idea is beautiful—at first. During this time, I tend to overlook all of ways that new exciting idea in its infancy is going to cause problems for me later. I once wrote a play with 20+ characters (not even main characters) who all had speaking parts. On paper, it was beautiful. Execution was a completely different matter. As time goes on, as you get into little disagreements with your project, you start to recognize that underneath all that cuteness is a bit of a mess. It's going to challenge you to grow and change if you stay with it. Sometimes, it is going to require more of you than you were perhaps willing to give. This includes the time commitment to get all those details right. At this point, it can be easier to just leave. It's easier to just fold up shop and start something new. But that's not where your victory is, Finisher.

It makes me think of Beyoncé's Coachella performance. It was gorgeous. It was captivating. But after watching the behind the scenes and seeing all the work that went into, it really drove this point home for me. There was attention to detail. Four months of rehearsals. And the dedication of time. There were 200+ people up on that stage, all with their own costumes and choreography, and yet they all needed to merge together for one cohesive performance. In the idea/honeymoon phase, I'm sure it sounded wonderful. When that idea has to be lived with day in and day out, when those relationship issues start, that's when the rubber meets the road. When I first watched the performance, I thought it was epic. After seeing the work involved, I finally understood *why* it was epic.

Those who need perfection to complete something or even stay involved with it are never going to finish anything. Nothing and nobody is perfect. Not that project you're currently working on. Not that relationship you're in. Not that church you go to. Not that person you married. Not you. Not even Beyoncé. (Yes, yes. I know the #hive thinks differently). Linked to any good or godly thing is always going to be stress, mistakes, annoyances, and push-back. Don't throw the baby out with the dirty bath water.

STICK WITH IT.

Anything worth having is going to be flawed and messy. These letters to you are flawed and messy. But I have to trust the editing process and that the first draft of a thing is not the final draft.

Finishing is going to take several drafts, edits, and forms. Hardly anything comes out exemplary the first time out. Every project needs tweaks. Our problem is that we want perfected versions of everything we get involved with. We want it fully formed right at the beginning. And unreasonable expectations are the surest way to discontent. Exercise patience while God is taking a red pen to the projects of your life, especially when the project is you. There's a perfecting that's taking place, and the version that's coming is indeed a finished (not a perfect) product.

P.S. What creative pursuit have you put down because of 'relationship issues'? Make a list of what those issues are and ask yourself, "Is it worth terminating completely?" Is there a way to work through the issues and keep the relationship?

32
The Fear Factor

"Fear defeats more people than any other one thing in the world."
Ralph Waldo Emerson

"Fear Sucks."
Candace Wilkins

Dear Finisher,

Throughout all these letters, I've hinted of my issues with fear. So much so that I wondered if I needed to dedicate an entire letter to it. But I figured since I've almost dedicated my entire creative life to it, a letter might be in order.

In 2017, I quietly decided that, similar to writer and TV show creator Shonda Rhimes, I would have my own "Year of Yes." I decided that every opportunity that came my way—ones that I'd ordinarily say no to out of fear—I would A) Probe why I was scared to do it, and B) Do it. This had me applying for jobs I was totally unqualified for. I went LIVE on FB for 30 days because I was challenged to do it. I worked with a well-known blogger/influencer as one of her assistants for an event. She told me my job was to do Insta-Stories to chronicle the event. Did I know how to do that? I sure didn't. And I was completely intimidated by the notion! Of course, the ugly voice of doubt had me kicking myself! Why didn't I volunteer for the registration table?! But I pressed on. I had a friend train me on the particulars, and the night before, I taught myself how to use it! I made it work! That same year, I also started writing three books. Yes, three. So needless to say, my "Year of Yes" was pretty lit. (Thanks, Shonda!) Every bit of what I accomplished started with me making a conscious decision to punch fear in the throat.

You have to understand, Finisher, fear has been my constant companion for many years. It's wrapped me up more times than I care to count. I used to think I had to just overwhelm it with courage, and then I'd conquer it. That in that single moment, fear would be banished to the far-reaches of the earth never to be heard or seen from again!

Umm, sure.

My "Year of Yes" was absolutely courageous. I daily overwhelmed my fear with my courage. When I decided to do a live teaching series on FB and IG for 30 days, I was *beyond* scared the first day! But every day, I was less and less fearful. By Day 30, I was an old hat at video! I remember thinking to myself, "Now you'll be able to do those IG stories you see everyone doing!" But have I done it? Nope. Why not? Because I'm scared. The courage I had to do the teaching series would not be the same courage I would need to do the next thing. I thought I was through with this fear thing! Nope. I'm still scared.

Here's a thought: Perhaps I have never addressed the underlying disease of my fear. Maybe I've merely dealt with the symptoms. I literally did an exercise to dig deeper into what was going on with me. I'll share that exercise with you.

What is the thing you are scared to do?	
Record the IG/FB stories	
Why?	**What don't you like about video?**
I don't know how to work it.	*People will be looking at me.*
So what?	**So what?**
I'd have to learn something new.	*I don't like how I currently look.*
Why is that a problem?	**What's the worst thing that can happen?**
It would be "on the job" training.	
Dig Deeper	
People will see if I make a mistake.	*People will make fun of me: the way I talk, look, act, and what I say.*
Why is this so terrible?	
I don't like public embarrassment.	
Define and Combine:	
I will be exposed. Existing in open view. Feelings of self-conscious shame and awkwardness.	
So what is your real fear?	
I'm scared that my internal fear and awkwardness – all the ways I'm self-conscious – will be in permanent and open view.	

Drill down to what your real fears are and attack them there. Don't waste energy dealing with symptoms. At the base of my fear of doing the social media videos were my most intimate insecurities. I feared that my closely guarded secrets would be on display for the world to see. It's the same reason I've always hated those prophetic lines in churches. What if the prophet sees something in me and blows up my spot in front of the whole church?! It's the same reason why, despite being a licensed minister, I loathe public speaking. It's also the same reason I hated high school. It felt like open season on my secret shames.

So what do we do about these deep-rooted fears? How do we conquer them? I honestly don't know that conquering the fear is the issue. For me, I found that dealing with the insecurity that the fear feeds on was most important. There is also a "B" side to those fears, too. My fears and insecurities have made me a more compassionate human being. As a minister who speaks prophetically to people, you will NOT catch me publicly blasting anyone! I am sensitive to people's internal struggles and brokenness because I'm dealing with my own. Now, that doesn't mean I always fall on the right side of kindness. Folks do irk me. But more often than not, I reach for grace first. A friend of mine has even coined the phrase "Hail Candace, full of Grace," a spin-off of the common Catholic prayer about Mary, mother of Jesus.

So even after we address the fear and deal with the underlying insecurity feeding it, does it go away? Not quite. 2 Timothy 1:7 says, "For God has not given us a spirit of fear, but of power, and of love and of a sound mind." Fear isn't just a mindset. It's a spirit. I heard popular pastor, Eugene Cho, once say "If God didn't give you the spirit of fear, who gave it to you?" I have often asked that question of myself. If it's not from God, there's only one other option—that ole trifling, bald-headed, slue-footed, productivity inhibitor. The devil is a liar! If I think of fear as a spirit from the devil himself, it makes it easier to stop playing patty-cake with it. Fear isn't my companion. It's something to be violently opposed to. Even in that, the devil isn't going to just let up. But it's one of those "objects in the mirror may appear larger than they are" kind of things. When the spirit of fear starts rearing its ugly head, take that as a sign that you're about to wreck shop! Every single time I've encountered the spirit of fear, the only thing that made it back up is doing the very thing it was trying to scare out of me. I ascended the pulpit and took the mic (hand shaking, but I did it.) I started the blog. I had the audacity to start a business where people paid me to consult at their churches. I'm writing this book.

The cure for fear isn't just confronting your issues and having the courage to face them—it's action! Do what scares you, Finisher! JUST DO IT! Take it from a pro. Once you start doing it, fear will no longer have a stronghold in that area. But here's the good and bad part about moving forward. Forward movement and fear go hand in hand. Whenever there's movement into an area of unfamiliarity, fear will round the corner and knock on the door. Your choice is whether you let it come in and kick up its feet.

P.S. Using my graphic as a guide, create your own for the fears in your life. Drill down what insecurities are feeding the fear. Start to attack that fear at the root.

33
Forgive to Finish

*"Let God deal with the things they do
'cause hate in your heart will consume you too."*
– Prophet Willard Carrol Smith Jr.

Dear Finisher,

I've recently been thinking about what it will look like when the projects I currently have on the table are finished and "successful." How will people in my life react? I thought about the people who didn't always do right by me. What will be their response? And for a second, a smile crept across my face. I imagined myself saying to all those people who treated me badly, who didn't see my gifts and abilities, who wrote me off, "How you like me now?"

Let's be honest, Finishers.

It feels good to *get back* at people who haven't always recognized you as the blessing you are. We feel especially justified when we didn't repay evil for evil in the moment, when we kept the receipts in our wallet, when we had the deck ready but didn't pull cards. Trust me, I get it. If I'm honest, I've been on the receiving end of some not-so-nice stuff from friends, family, places of employment, and yes, places of worship. I remember an ex-boyfriend of mine who dumped me while we were planning to attend a big event together. Not only did he end the relationship abruptly, but he immediately started dating another girl (who I suspect he was seeing while dating me). I wanted revenge so bad that I worked for over a year to make him want me back. And it worked. Once he wanted me back, I was already in love with someone else. Ha! Take that! But to be honest, the time it took to enact revenge against him and the girl who "took him" (which I wholeheartedly don't believe in – no one can *take* a grown man), was ultimately not worth it. I regret it to this day. My authentic self isn't confrontational so, yes, I've often been the receptacle for some pretty trash behavior. And yes, I absolutely know what it's like to just want to take that knife of worldly success and just "stick it" to those folks. But after that episode and even as those thoughts come up in passing now, God chin-checks me. Hard.

God had me read a passage of scripture that got me *all* the way together. If you know the story of Joseph in the bible, you know that Joseph was a young guy with a dream from God (and his father's favorite) who was treated horrifically by those closest to him. Let me give you the quick and dirty rundown. Joseph's brothers conspired to kill him, threw him in a pit, and sold him into slavery. Even while in slavery, God was with Joseph, and he rose to prominence in Potiphar's house. But then, Potiphar's wife kept trying to seduce him and, eventually, falsely accused him of rape. He was then jailed for a crime he didn't commit. While there, he became a dream interpreter for other prisoners with a promise that he would be remembered when one of the prisoners got out. He wasn't. He stayed in jail until Pharaoh had a dream that needed interpretation. Once Joseph correctly interpreted the dream, Pharaoh set him as governor over all of Egypt, second only to Pharaoh himself. He was able to prepare Egypt for an oncoming famine that hit the land. So here's where it gets *really* interesting. Famine also hit Canaan (where Joseph's family lived), and Joseph's brothers made their way to Egypt to buy food. They all eventually stood before Joseph, and after passing a series of tests, Joseph revealed himself as their long-lost brother. Eventually, their father passed away, and then we get this nugget of scripture that almost brought me to tears. Genesis 50:15-21 says,

> *"15 When Joseph's brothers saw that their father was dead, they said, "What if Joseph carries a grudge against us and pays us back in full for all the wrong which we did to him?" 16 So they sent word to Joseph, saying, "Your father commanded us before he died, saying, 17 'You are to say to Joseph, "I beg you, please forgive the transgression of your brothers and their sin, for they did you wrong."' Now, please forgive the transgression of the servants of the God of your father." And Joseph wept when they spoke to him. 18 Then his brothers went and fell down before him [in confession]; then they said, "Behold, we are your servants (slaves)." 19 But Joseph said to them, "Do not be afraid, for am I in the place of God? [Vengeance is His, not mine.] 20 As for you, you meant evil against me, but God meant it for good in order to bring about this present outcome, that many people would be kept alive [as they are this day]. 21 So now, do not be afraid; I will provide for you and support you and your little ones." So he comforted them [giving them encouragement and hope] and spoke [with kindness] to their hearts."*

Verse 19 took me out, Finishers. Joseph asked, "Am I in the place of God?" In reading this, God spoke something to my heart. Joseph was in the position to rain down all manner of vengeance on his brothers, and technically, it would have been justified. They did some terrible things to him, right? He was in position, but it wasn't his PLACE. Do you see that? Sometimes, finishing can put you in a particular position, and what you do in that position of power is the real test of your character. Let me tell you a great indication of when you're ready for the #FinishersPosition: when you can forgive folks and use the same position to bless them who tried to curse you! I recently made a list of people I needed to forgive. These were people I needed to release from the shackles of my own notions of vengeance. Because that's the part we don't often pay attention to in Joseph's story. We're down with Deuteronomy 32:35, "Vengeance is Mine, and recompense; Their foot shall slip in due time; For the day of their calamity is at hand, And the things to come hasten upon them."

We can get with God getting our enemies back—as long as He does it the way we want. As long as that calamity comes upon them quickly and in our full view! But what happens if the story just ends with you blessing them? Can we handle that, Finisher? Can we be like Joseph and provide for them and speak a blessing over them? Can we trust that maybe our forgiveness is playing a part in God's larger story than our vengeance ever could?

When God made me make that list of people I needed to forgive, I was confused because I thought some of those people I had already forgiven. I said, "Well, I don't speak badly of them in public. I'm not mad anymore." But God said to me, "You've feigned forgiveness for public consumption but not really in your heart." If I'm still fantasizing about *sticking it to them* when I get a 'position,' then that forgiveness isn't real. Vengeance isn't my place. It's not your place either. That's hard, right? Our finishing is not a way to get back at anyone. It's not what we want to hear. But honestly, holding onto unforgiveness keeps you a perpetual victim. You'll make decisions out of your pain, not your power. I don't want that. I don't want to *act* gracious. I want to move in spaces I was kicked out of and *be* gracious knowing this truth: what they may have meant for evil God meant for my good. That good brought about my present outcome.

Can we rest in the fact that any evil perpetuated against us can be used for our good to bring about God's ultimate outcome? That's much easier to digest looking backward. Sure, we can look at our past and say, "Yes. God used it." But can we look forward with a hindsight perspective and keep God's outcome ever before us? And let's be clear: the outcome isn't just the position, it's who we become getting to that position. Joseph had some character development and growing to do from that young lad with those outrageous dreams. God spent time cultivating Joseph's gifts, drilling humility and trust into him, and training him to be Egypt's governor. He needed every bit of it.

Stop resisting God's journey for you, Finisher. If you get thrown into the proverbial pit, try to keep the bigger outcome in mind. Where you're going and who you'll be when you get there is what really matters. Let's not try to get into a finisher's position only to try to take God's place. Repaying folks with evil is too small a purpose to serve and only reveals our small-mindedness. It tells us we're not yet ready to be "Egypt's governor." We're not yet ready to serve the masses and keep people alive, especially if we're going to be gate-keepers. Joseph got into the position to bless a whole country, the surrounding area, and the very family that flung him out. If we're finishing to hoard our blessings over other folk, to stand at the gate and only serve those who haven't hurt us, we're not yet ready to receive what God has for us.

Wow! Did I just write that? God help me. That truth hurts even me. Friend, let's just forgive so we can finish.

P.S. Make that list of people you need to forgive and then actively work on forgiving them. In your heart.

34
Expect Attack

"Two times that attack is greatest; when purpose is about to be revealed and when purpose is about to be fulfilled."
Bishop Walter Scott Thomas

Dear Finisher,

Anytime you're attempting to put anything out into the world that has purpose beyond you, get ready for the fight of your life! While I know it's cliché to say, it doesn't make it any less true. Be prepared for everything in life to blow up, everything that can go wrong to go wrong, and all the people in your life to hit high levels of act-right deficiency. I had a deadline to hit this week, and of course, as if on schedule, tomfoolery ensued. Hubby and I were sniping at each other all week, my body straight revolted health-wise, and every distraction that you could possibly think of flung itself in my path. At this point, I should expect it, I suppose. Whenever it's time for us to reap any size harvest, whenever it's time to receive what we've been praying about, when you've just gotten clarity on purpose, when you're all ready, set, go about your promise, expect the enemy of your soul to let loose!

I remember a time about a decade ago when my writing juices were flowing heavily. As I shared, I wrote plays previously. One play in particular was so well received by the community that people wanted it to go on tour. So I sat down and began revising the script. I added new characters, new plot twists, etc. For a few weeks, I stayed up late, grinding out page after page. I was so excited. I got up to 40 pages of new dialogue. I saved it to a flash drive. Not too long after that, I went to open the file, and it wasn't there. It was gone. Totally gone. It was the only file missing from the drive.

I never recovered it.

(You feel that? That's me. My heart is screaming even all these years later.)

I was so distraught after losing all that work that I didn't write anything for TEN years. Every time I would sit down in front of a blank screen, all I could remember was those 40 lost forever pages. You won't convince me that losing that file was random. It was too calculated. That one act helped me impede my own progress.

The enemy has no intentions of allowing you to freely walk into whatever God has for you. He is going to pull out all the stops, and we need to be prepared. Some of us are never going to finish because we fall back every time the enemy mounts an assault against us. The enemy can't stop you; he can only make forward movement difficult. He can only divert your attention so that you're not keeping the main thing. Remember, the thief comes only to steal, kill, and destroy.

Prior to even starting these letters, I was challenged by a friend to go live on FB to do a 30-day teaching series. There I was, trying to do 30 days of teaching with my track record of not finishing things. And for 30 days, the enemy's assault was varied and methodical. He used some old faithful tactics and new ones I hadn't encountered yet. He used fear, intimidation, sickness, neck pain, fatigue, apathy, depression, and more. It was a rough 30 days. But, despite it all, I pushed through. I got on live for 30 days. And if I'm honest, I don't know that if I hadn't conquered those 30 days, that I would have been able to write these letters. I suppose God knew I would need a recent memory of finishing to hold on to. So you see, the enemy wasn't just trying to stop those 30 live videos, he was trying to further solidify his version of who I was—a non-finisher and prevent this book from ever existing. If I couldn't commit to 30 live videos, what would make me think I could finish a book?

Two years ago, God started impressing upon me how important it was to start spending daily time with Him. I had been slacking. He kept pushing me. I knew he was preparing me for something. He needed me to build up an arsenal with which to fight.

I've needed every bit of that arsenal as I've taken on this project.

See, we are too often playing checkers while the enemy is playing chess. He is strategic. As my deadlines have closed in, the harder it's felt to write. I've been fighting laziness, apathy, sickness, boredom, and creativity blocks. Sure, husbands and wives fight, and it could just be random. But I do find it interesting that the month before this book is due, my husband and I have been at each other's throats. One day I was so upset by a disagreement, I didn't write all day. And there it is.

We cannot be ignorant of the enemy's devices. At least we shouldn't be. We can't afford to be. If we're going to finish, we have to know that premeditated opposition will come our way, *and* we don't have to fall victim to those schemes. Let's start to see some of life's obstructions for what they really are—moves on the chessboard trying to ensure we lose the game. Now that

I know that this is what happens, I can fight differently and with intention. I can stop arguing with my husband because I'm not wrestling against flesh and blood (see Eph. 6:12). I don't have to succumb to every sickness because by His stripes I am healed (see Isaiah 53:5). I can start speaking words of life when feelings of death are trying to overtake me.

Finisher, use your energy to fight the real enemy.

P.S. Make a list of what happens every time you try to move forward in a particular area. Do you see any patterns? Start to pinpoint those areas in prayer.

35
What to Do

"Now what is we gon' do?"
Jay Bailey, prolific pontificator and friend

Dear Finisher,

So we're coming down to the last of these letters. It is my sincere prayer that they've been some help to you. Shoot, they've helped me! But I would be remiss if I didn't ask you, "What are you going to do?" Or maybe a better question is, "What have you done?" Has anything in this book prompted to you to take action?

Listen, if you've just been reading this book, nodding your head at different parts, highlighting, writing notes in the margins, and thinking deeply about all my P.S., but you haven't taken even a single action step toward your own healing, then all you have done is hitch a ride to my finish line.

And that's whack, Finisher.

I have been guilty of this. I have read the self-help/God-help/Somebody HELP books, been convicted by what they said, but never did anything about *what* they said. The thing that no one tells you about all those books is that *you* have to be ready. You have to be sick and tired of being sick and tired. You have to be ready to put a plan into action, and then YOU HAVE TO

DO IT. Whenever I've read those books over the years, I wasn't ready. I didn't want to be free. At least, not really. I preferred the coziness and familiarity of oppression. And I needed to be honest about that. Once I told myself the truth, I decided to not be that joker anymore. You know how you know you're done with a problematic ex? You stop looking at those old text messages. You block the number FOR REAL. You cut them off on social media. You stop communicating with them, and you fill your life with other stuff. No, I didn't just start writing this book. I had to cut #TheSpiritofDoNothing off like an ex. I had to cut off communication. When fear came knocking, I had to push past it, not just pray. I had to do weird things that seemed like they had nothing to do with writing this book. I had to put myself in uncomfortable spaces when I didn't know a soul, buy a book of writing prompts to get juices flowing, take a class at a church way across town for nine months in a ministry gift I was scared to death to truly acknowledge, meet with my pastor about moving into ministry, go live on FB for 30 days straight, etc. There was a lot that happened before I put one finger on this keyboard. All of it was absolutely necessary to get these pages out. All of them were steps. The first step was me losing my job. That took care of my time excuse. What else did I have to do but write?

I want to say this to those who identify as believers who are reading this. I have been to *all* the church conferences. I have been laid out at the altar crying. I have preached to others while simultaneously disqualifying myself. I have prayed and asked God to take it away. I've had all the prophetic words spoken to and over me. None of it made a difference until I took action. Sometimes as believers, we spend so much time running from conference to conference, praying and snotting, doing work in the church building that we neglect the work that God is trying to do in *His church* (us). Faith without works is dead (see James 2:17). We're out here dragging corpses to church every Sunday. Dragging them up to the choir loft or behind the mic on the praise team. Dragging them down the center aisle when we usher. Dragging them up on the pulpit and letting them preach! If your Holy Ghost only makes you cry, it's a faucet, not a Helper. If your faith only works at the conference, but doesn't help you to take action after you leave, is it location-contingent? If the Word of the Lord comes to you in tongues but won't come to you in the form of a to-do list, keep it! The Holy Spirit is a counselor. The Holy Spirit is a helper. What are we doing for the Holy Spirit to provide us with counsel or help?! What ground have we taken for the cause of Christ? God told Joshua, "Wherever your foot treads is yours!" We quote the scripture, but won't move our feet! How much finishing have we forfeited?

We keep talking about the "the devil." Everything is not the devil. In truth, we aren't even doing enough for the devil to resist! We blame the devil and confine our worship to church on Sundays or private devotion in our homes. Stop thinking of worship one-dimensionally. Worship with your actions! Worship by letting God use every gift He's put in you. We are wasting what God has put in us! It's a tragedy! We out here worrying about not having sex, not cussing people out, and checking off these "I'm a good Christian" lists. Meanwhile, we're out here grieving the Holy Spirit with our inaction!

P.S. Write down three action steps you can take toward finishing. Better yet, take action on the 34 other P.S. you've already received. Hmph!

36
Trust the Process

"The magic you're looking for is in the work you're avoiding."
Anonymous

Dear Finisher,

I've been praying and thinking about next steps lately. Honestly, I've been reluctant to even entertain such notions because I'm struggling to finish *this* step! Bringing these letters over the finish line has seemingly taken all the strength I have. But once I finish, then what? As I said before, finishing is really about reaching the next start line of a new race. Most of us never prepare to finish. We never prepare for our harvest. We don't do what we can do while waiting on what only God can do. We hardly give God anything to work with.

I once prayed a prayer for all my debt to be wiped out. I didn't want to owe anybody anything. I wanted my credit score to go up, and I wanted every single debt to be paid off (especially school debt). I remember hearing a testimony of a lady at church that said she called to get on a payment plan for a huge credit card debt she owed, and they said she didn't owe anything. So I prayed, and I said God, "Wipe it out! I have faith! Do it!" So, I waited. And waited. No wipe out happened. And I was low-key angry about it. Okay, high-key. Why doesn't this stuff ever work for me? Then God gathered my whole life. He reminded me that the lady called the credit company to get on a payment plan. Had I done that?

Well, no.

"I can't afford to even get on a payment plan. I don't make enough, God!"

Unh huh. Okay, well, have you worked on being more fiscally responsible? How do I know if I wipe your debt out you won't end up in the same spot this time next year?

"Because I won't!"

Good answer. So, you say you can't afford to pay on your debts. Not even a little bit. But you CAN afford that pair of shoes you had to have last week?

"I don't want to talk about this anymore."

Stop laughing.

If God promised us delicious homemade spaghetti for dinner a year from now, what would be our expectation? Would our expectation be that a bowl of spaghetti would just appear on our table around dinner time? For some of us, the answer is yes. And if God chose to do it that way, it certainly *could* happen. I mean He is God and all. But more than likely, that's not the way it's going down. More than likely, God is going to remind us about that plot of land behind the house that has good soil — good tomato growing soil. When you go to the store to grab those tomato seeds, you'll probably find that all the gardening tools are half off as it's the end of the season. When you get up to the checkout counter, you might encounter the customer service representative who has a garden of her own. She'll give you all the tips/tricks on how best to grow those tomatoes, and because she just feels a kinship with you, she'll throw in onion and bell pepper seeds just to be nice. When you get home to till that ground, you might just find that it's easier than you thought it'd be. Probably because of those tools you thought you couldn't afford but were on sale. You plant those seeds in the ground and hope it works out. You follow the directions that your new gardening friend suggested and...wait, one second now, nothing grows.

Yep. You read that right.

Nothing grows.

You're so disappointed. How could it not have worked? You call your friend, and she laughs at you. She tells you that it's not the right season for those seeds to grow, that what you're growing must take root below before it shows up to the outside world. It will take some time, and some rain. But she tells you that while you're waiting, protect what you're growing and be patient. She tells you that sometimes frost will come, and the weather won't always cooperate with what you're trying to grow.

You'll start to see buds, and excitement fills you! Gardening homie (because of course you're homies now) tells you to purchase some type of wire to keep animals from trying to snatch up what you're growing. She says that your buds are at a very vulnerable stage. You realize that you're starting to grow weary of taking care of these plants. You want that spaghetti dinner that God promised you over all of this work. You don't want any more advice from your new gardener friend. It seems like a lot of work just for the spaghetti dinner that *God* promised you. Or, is it?

P.S. For every prayer you have before God currently, write out three practical steps you can take.

37
The Decoys

"Don't fall for the decoy!"
Minister Candace Tucker (also known as me)

Dear Finisher,

So, you're over it, huh?

You think there must be an easier way to get that delicious spaghetti dinner. You decide to run to Target (because all answers to life are found in Target), and you find a whole entire section of spaghetti sauces. All different types. And you think to yourself, "I didn't have to grow my own vegetables. All I have to do is buy this jar. It's the same thing."

Oh but, dear Finisher, it's not. That jar of sauce may be all right, but it's not *quite* what God promised. That jar has got extra preservatives that are probably bad for you. It's not going to taste as fresh as those tomatoes growing in your backyard. Sure, it's quicker. Sure, it won't require all the work, but it's not *quite* what God promised. He promised a homemade delicious spaghetti dinner.

Sometimes on this finishing journey, it's easier to take the decoy. We talked about taking the easy way out earlier, but this is different because often in doing the hard thing of trusting God's process, we accept what I call the Decoy Promise. It's not *quite* what God spoke. It's not even *quite* what you want. But it doesn't require any more from you. It stops that crazy waiting game. It gives you the immediate gratification without what you perceive to be the stifling process. And…it makes a mess of everything.

Look at Abram and Sarai in Genesis (see Gen 15-16). God promised them an heir. He promised them that it would come, but they decided it was taking too long, so they decided to help God out. Sarai gave her servant Hagar to Abram so that she could "build a family through her." Finisher, can I tell you something? You can't build what God promised with tools that God didn't sanction. God doesn't need your help and won't be rushed! We out here trying to build with the wrong tools and then wondering why we're not getting the results that God promised. Jarred spaghetti sauce isn't what God promised *you*. It *is* someone else's promise though. Someone did the work to get that jar to those shelves, but that isn't your finish line. How many of us have taken someone else's work and try to pass it off as what God promised you?

We're doing all this because we're trying to avoid the process and who God is making us into during it. I told you before you can't get to your finish line trying to run someone else's race. Don't accept decoys, Finishers. Trust me, when the process is the hardest, when you're tired and overwhelmed, when you're exhausted of running the race, that Target run to those shelves full of jarred sauce will feel completely justified. The enemy of your soul will float every possible decoy in front of your face. And things that you never would have accepted previously will start looking like a prize.

I know, I know. I hear you. "I mean, what is really wrong with jarred spaghetti sauce? It's good for millions of people, right? It can't be totally wrong. If it works for others, why can't it work for me?"

Here's the thing: we usually aren't seeking out jarred sauce because we believe it's God's best. We accept it because the alternative is difficult. Imagine having to watch everyone eat their own spaghetti dinners in your face when you just planted your tomato seeds in the ground?

I once saw a lady in a business FB group try and steal another lady's idea. She tried to steal everything down to the branding, marketing hashtags, labels, and font choice. She started marketing her items, and they so closely resembled that people started purchasing her stuff because they thought she was affiliated with the original. Quickly, two things happened. 1) People received the product and while it *looked* like the original, they quickly deduced that the items were indeed *not* the original. One comment said, "The quality wasn't on par with the original." 2) The "decoy" company received a cease and desist from the original company with a threat of litigation.

She quickly dismantled her business.

That lady wanted the harvest of what the original company had taken many years and resources to build from scratch. Instead of her waiting for her own seeds to sprout, she went poking (and poaching) around in someone else's garden. And while she tried to duplicate what she saw to reap the harvest, she couldn't. Because decoys can never be originals, no matter how hard they try.

Or how hard we squint.

Waiting for seeds to sprout takes patience and faith. It takes stamina and a strong internal fortitude to submit to doing something God's way despite external pressure to cower.

Finishers don't cower to people (and maybe even your own mind) and end up grabbing what God is calling you to grow! You've got seeds in the ground, Finisher! Just keep preparing for the rain.

P.S. In what ways have you settled for decoys (trying to rush God) in your own life instead of being patient with your seeds? Write them out and then ~~cross them out~~ and resolve to wait for your seeds to grow.

38
Prepare for Rain

"Rain only matters to those who have seed in the ground/I've got seed in the ground/I'm expecting a harvest now"
William McDowell

Dear Finisher,

I'm so glad we decided to leave that jarred spaghetti sauce on the shelf, aren't you? (If it's still in your hands, put it down!) Well, maybe you're not glad. At least not yet. And I get it. You're still waiting for those seeds to mature, and you're getting hungry! The gardener friend of yours has been counseling you about all that you've planted from the tomatoes, onions, and peppers to the herb seeds you decided to grab on a whim. You've got so much in the ground, Finisher. Maybe you only have one chapter left in your dissertation. Maybe you're almost done with the grant application or business plan. Maybe your website is almost ready to go live. Maybe you've lost twenty of the 40 pounds you want to lose. Maybe you're almost done your book (smiles at self).

Now what? God has promised a homemade, delicious spaghetti dinner. God has promised you that your business will be successful or that book will bless plenty of people. Are you just supposed to sit around and wait for everything to grow? I was watching a movie once, and a man told a story about two farmers who were desperate for rain for their crops, but only one went out and prepared his fields to receive it. Who do you think trusted and believed God for the rain? Yes. The one who prepared. If God promised you that spaghetti dinner, what have you done besides plant those vegetables and herbs? There is more to a spaghetti dinner than tomatoes. You need knives to cut those tomatoes, pots to cook sauce in, and pasta to serve with the sauce. What have you done to prepare for the tasks that need to occur after finishing? Have you thought about it?

Maybe you're so consumed with trying to finish and thinking you don't have time to think about what happens afterward. Is the inability to #planforward an indication of a lack of time or a lack of belief that you'll actually have anything to plan for? Come on, Finisher! We're close! The tomatoes are ripening! Don't let doubt start creeping in! Even while I'm writing these letters to you, I'm planning past them. I'm asking God for the strategy and next steps. How do I let people know about these letters? How do I protect myself? Who are the right people to come alongside me in this next season of life? And I'm not just looking at the outward strategies. I've spent more time in prayer and with God seeking help with shaping my character to handle the ascent. And as soon as I secure more of the bag, I am going to therapy!

Yep, therapy.

Because beyond making money, the biggest bag we need to secure is ourselves! Listen, there's a whole spaghetti dinner you were promised! You better get to planning for it! You can't wait until the tomatoes are ripe, and it's time to harvest what you've planted to think about what you're going to be using the tomatoes for. Think about it while they're growing. Dust that recipe book God gave you off the shelf and make sure you've got all the ingredients on-hand. Start chopping. Start cooking. You can just taste it, can't you, Finisher? I legit smell it. I can smell that sweet sauce filling my nostrils. I can taste that hot Italian sausage and that tablespoon of sugar I add (Hush: this is *my* recipe!). I've set the table beautifully, and I'm ready to eat.

Starting this book was me putting my seeds in the ground. Continuing to write was cultivating the soil, taking care of what I put in the ground. Praying was akin to protecting my growing buds with fencing. My gardening homie was the Holy Spirit instructing me. Following the recipe was me reading my Word and hearing from God about what the Spirit wanted revealed in this book. My table setting is my publisher, marketing, copyright protection, etc.

It's time to eat.

Imagine my surprise when I sit my proverbial dinner down in front of me, and I realize that there are eight more place settings. I envision Jesus asking me who I've invited.

Huh? I didn't think to invite anyone.

He says, "That's an awful lot of spaghetti for just us." I guess I just figured I'd eat leftovers—you know, eat off my hard work for a little bit. But Jesus' promises are to be shared.

Oh.

Finisher, that product you're trying to finish? That God-thing? If it's just serves you, it's too small. I would also question if it's a God-thing at all. God's promises always serves a larger purpose than your desires, needs, and appetite. That project/purpose/product is to be shared. If you're eating, and no one in your community is, that's a problem. If you're one of those who believes, "I don't need nobody but me and Jesus," you're not astute or prolific—you're hurt. Life is to be lived in community. Finishing should be bigger than you. Crossing your finish line should bring others to their own finish line. It should inspire, cajole, maybe even drag, but it should definitely do more than serve you. God's promises are never single-serve.

P.S. Let that last sentence marinate. Is what you're asking God for single-serve? If it is, A. Ask yourself if it's serving God or your ego. B. If it's a God-vision, expand its reach. Think of ways that it can serve those who are beyond just you.

39
Finishing Well

"It is easier to begin well than to finish well."
Plautus

Dear Finisher,

I told you when I began these letters to you, I wasn't sure I'd finish them. I told you, in my mind, my finishing track record wasn't positive. Do you know how many times I've sat down to write a book? How many years people have been asking me when my book was coming out? I would open my laptop to a blank page, and nothing would come out. I tried to force it. I'd start. Then I'd stop. I prayed. I cried. It's one of the worst feelings ever to know you're capable of doing something, to know you're gifted, to know you're SUPPOSED to do it, and yet…can't. Even with this project, there were moments when I didn't think I'd make it. I was passionate about it. It felt like something I was supposed to do. It felt like a God-project. The few people who knew I was writing this book were beyond excited to read it, even asking for the raw unedited version before I even sent it to the publisher. I heard "about time" more than I care to admit. And yet there were days, even after outlining chapters, even after I had written some good stuff, I wasn't sure these letters would ever see the light of day.

The principles in these letters aren't cute little self-help anecdotes. They are principles I've had to believe and live out. The days when I wanted to bury myself under the covers and cry myself to sleep were the days I opened my laptop while tears slipped down my cheeks. The days my husband challenged me about being lackadaisical were the days I opened my laptop and angrily pounded the keys until a chapter poured out. When someone asked me where I was working, and I felt ashamed that I didn't have a "real" job, so I said, "I'm working on my business," and they gave me that "She ain't doing nothing with her life" look, I came home and wrote. When I wanted a job because I was tired of being broke and not financially contributing to my home, God shut every door. The only open door was an opened laptop. The day I had a mental breakdown in Walmart (tears and all) because I was calculating how much Oreos would put me over my budget, I wrote. When I no longer recognized my own life, I wrote. For all the times my friends went on trips, and I couldn't go because I couldn't afford it, I pushed myself to write. "Let my absence from the *good life* not be in vain, Lord," I prayed. The days I got distracted for hours with YouTube, only to beat myself up relentlessly for being what I perceived to be a fraud turned into me killing the game the next day writing two or three chapters.

I turned down other creative pursuits because I had to remain focused. I had to be willing to let other people pour into me. I'm so grateful for friends who paid for movies, dinners, Starbucks, and free tickets to events in other states when I couldn't afford to pay for gas or tolls or even put money in on the snacks. When I realized I couldn't pay them back, and my pride was officially dead, and guilt overran me, I opened my laptop because those same friends told me that the only payment they wanted from me was a finished book. When my mentor asked for my help at an event that I suspect she didn't need me for but just wanted to make sure I was in the room with beautiful black women creatives who could inspire me (and she could throw me a couple dollars without *giving* me a couple dollars), I went home and wrote if only to make them proud.

Somewhere along the way, I realized that the project that needed to be finished wasn't this book, it was me. God had been trying to do an important work in me, and I'd been resistant because I was scared. I feared how much it would hurt, how much it'd expose me. I thought, *how many issues would need to be unearthed to finish this project?* I told you, my greatest fear is that my internal shame, awkwardness, and all the ways I'm self-conscious would be in permanent open view. I've been in hiding for so long I didn't know how to be seen. This book (whether it's read by one or one million) would make me seen. I spent more than a decade at a job complaining about how they didn't see me for all my gloriousness, yet the truth was I was really scared of my own light. God said to me, "You can't finish *it* because you won't let Me finish (my work in) you." While I was finishing these letters to you, God was in the operating room, finishing the surgery I kept rescheduling. He opened my heart and ripped apart my flesh. He started ridding me of pride, selfishness, passive-aggressive behavior, self-sabotage, the fear that my gaffes would always overrule and overtake my giftedness, and my belief that I was destined to become a vat of wasted potential. I thought I was just writing you these letters, but God was rewriting some truths over my heart.

Dear Finisher, it's not just about finishing, but it's more about finishing well. These letters to you weren't just about changing our external behaviors so that we'd look better to the outside world. Can I tell you something you may not want to hear? Finishing never ends. Once you finish "the thing," the "next thing" needs to be finished. It doesn't mean we don't celebrate, but it does mean we don't stagnate. I'm less concerned with you finishing the thing in front of you and more concerned with cultivating your belief in yourself as a finisher. Finishing is a behavior, a solitary act. Believing yourself to *be* a finisher is what allows that one act to happen over and over again. It's a belief that stretches you from what you do to who you are. Writing these letters to you have really transformed me and my thinking. When I first started, it really was about finishing this project. I started with one line: "I hope I finish this book." That was the paramount result I was shooting for. But somewhere along the way, it became less about zeroing in on this one finish line. I didn't just want this one result. I wanted to covenant with the process of who I am becoming—a finisher who finishes. Writing these letters to you, letting God take me on this journey, has yielded unexpected results. It hasn't been easy. It's required more of me than I initially thought. They've certainly made me walk out what I talk.

God is taking me some place. I don't know where. But for years, God has been telling me to get off the shore. To get in the boat. To launch out into the deep. I've been beckoned to walk on water. And each time, I get closer, I dip my toe in and run right back in the opposite direction. I'm now convinced that it isn't the act of walking on water that God's impressed with; it's the inner fortitude, the faith, the audacity to believe we could. That we could do something that everything and everyone around us (including ourselves) deems impossible.

I also recently realized a scary fact: my personal view of God was shaped in my image. I'd been worshipping a God that looks, acts, and responds like I do. A God who is a harsh critic. One who is fearful of new beginnings. One who fears selfish ambition and yet covets it. A God who is double-minded, unstable in every way. That doesn't sound like the God of the Bible that I read. Is it any wonder that it was difficult for me to believe in the beckoning? To believe that God wanted me out *on* the ocean when I'd convinced myself that just getting to the beach was enough? Finisher, getting to your beach isn't enough. Finishing this one thing isn't enough. As I've said, each finish line is just the starting line to the next race. And maybe that's what wearies us. We know that each ending is just a new beginning, so we avoid finishing. We've never accepted that we're finishers, so all we can think about is not finishing before we even start.

Sound familiar? I'm not who I was when I started these letters to you. Every day that I've written, I'm changing. I've become a Finisher who finishes! There were no shortcuts through this process. I had to believe it, and I had to do it. I had to believe that I was a finisher that finished, and then, I had to finish. Bottom line. If you can't first believe and then do, you will keep showing up to the beach, but you'll never approach the water. You'll keep getting in position at the start line, but you'll cut out halfway through the race. You'll keep starting, but you won't finish. Believe that you can finish. Believe that God is with you. Believe that God put everything in you to be a finisher that finishes.

May we finish well and be well when we finish!

P.S. Finisher, you should have a notebook FULL of information. About yourself. About your plans. About the things that have *previously* hindered you and what you can do about it. Go. Do. Finish.

40
A Love Letter

"You yourselves are our letter of recommendation, written on our hearts, to be known and read by all."
2 Corinthian 3:2 ESV

My Dearest Finisher,

This is my final letter to you. I wasn't quite sure what else I had to say. I asked God to give me the exact words that we would need to push us to our own finish lines. This is what I heard:

"I, your God, am with you. The trouble you've encountered recently was there to reveal a larger truth that you keep trying to avoid. I've had a lot to say to you, but you keep silencing me. Please stop. When I said I wouldn't leave you or forsake you, I meant it. The problem you've been having is that you keep forsaking yourself. You don't think you're worth it. Oh, my dear heart, YOU ARE! You are more than even the work, projects, words, or service you render to the world. You are worth it not just for what you're DOING but just because of who you are. I don't count you worthy because you finished; I counted you worthy when I finished. You spend so much time chasing

after worthiness in pursuits that are really drawing you farther away from me. You are my beloved, whether you finish or not. You don't have to prove it to Me; I know who you are. I created you. The person that needs to know you can finish isn't Me, it's you. I'm not holding your past (10 years or 10 minutes) against you. You are, though. Free yourself of all your preconceived notions about who you are. Come to Me and let Me tell you what I had in mind all along for you. I can help you redeem the time. You are not late. You are not behind. Run the race I have set before you. Stay close to me, and I will not only reveal your original design, I will grant you the joy you so desperately need and has handily eluded you. I have come that you might have life and have it more abundantly. That isn't just about stuff, personal accomplishments, roles, and responsibilities. That is about believing that the Finished work on the cross has enough power to break the sin-sick habits of your life and the generational curses of your family. It's a belief that my finished work is enough to get you to your finished work. You are already a Finisher. Let me work in you so that you can become a finisher that finishes."

Welp. Fam, I finished. I finished this book. I have more hang-ups than a clothesline on a spring day, but I harvested my tomatoes. I followed the recipe God sent over, and I set the table for that delicious spaghetti dinner God promised. I just shared my spaghetti dinner with you, and now that you're full...go figure out what God promised you! Because if I can finish...

Acknowledgments

Crossing this particular finish line has been a hard-fought battle. I would not have made it without the support of so many people who cheered me on. First, to my publisher New Season Books & Media and its relentless, determined and dauntless leader Tracey M. Lewis-Giggetts. From the moment I told you of this idea, you were in. Pushing. Pulling. Driving me CRAZY. You are truly a mid-wife for creatives and a GIANT among women. You are the mentor I prayed for and the big sis I didn't even know I needed. I am forever indebted to you. #ItsHarvestTime

To LaGuardia Cross: thank you for being the catalyst! You said, "*That's* your first book!" And look! It is!

To my family, I thank you for the support and excitement for this work! For every Facebook share, every "That's my cousin!" post, every call and text, please know I appreciate and love you. To my aunties, Catherine Barnes and Cynthia Lambirth who helped raise me, helped shape me, and still get excited to see me when I come home—I thank you for always being sincere in your love for me, for not missing one important event in my life, for advocating for me behind the scenes with Mom, and for making your family, my family these last 3+ decades.

To my church family, Enon Tabernacle Baptist Church, thank you for loving me back to church life.

To the friends I've had since I landed in Philadelphia almost 20 years ago, The Divas. I thank you for the friendship, the lessons, the irritations, the call-outs, the prayers, the silence, the arguments, the laughs and the support. Always support, even when we're angry. I would not be here without ALL of it. Real

Talk? I'll always love you heffas—crazy though we may be. To the Core. In some ways, you've mothered me, fathered me, and sistered me. Thank you for deep-diving with me into my healing. Thank you for sometimes grabbing my hand and pulling me toward deep waters. Thank you for sometimes pulling me away from quicksand. Thank you for always knowing I was CAN-WIL even while I was CAN-TUCK (you'll get that on the way home).

To all the friends (new and old) who've been patiently waiting for this book and encouraging, praying and speaking life to me along the way. I have a beautiful network of sisterhood (and brotherhood), and I wouldn't trade it.

To my mom. For every sacrifice you've made on my behalf, every time you put me first, I thank you. To always "making it work." To making my childhood full of good memories, good people, good music, and good food. You are everybody's fave for good reason. I won't be embarrassed if you tell everybody about this accomplishment. Puff your chest all the way out. Call everyone!

To my husband, Hakiem T. Wilkins, there isn't any way this book would be here without you. You are legit God's biggest and best gift to me. You're the best thing I never knew I needed. I know how blessed I am. To have a partner who only wants you to be your best self, who only wants you to shine, who gets just as excited about the finished product as you do is a rarity indeed. You've never tried to dim my light, never tried to make me small so you could be large. You took on all the financial burdens so that I could focus on writing. Thank you for being more than my husband. Thank you for being my partner, my closest confidant, my most trusted advisor, and my staunchest ally. Love is too common a word. I Stedman you.

To my Maker & Master, Jesus Christ. I worship you with the words of this book.

I tell my story, and You get Glory.

"And they overcame and conquered him because of the blood of the Lamb and because of the word of their testimony..."
Revelation 12:11 AMP

Contact Candace E. Wilkins at
www.candacewilkins.com

CPSIA information can be obtained
at www.ICGtesting.com
Printed in the USA
BVHW032306160819
556097BV00001B/4/P